FATULOUS

A MEMOIR

FATULOUS

A MEMOIR

HEATHER REAM

KHAMIR PRESS

Knoxville, Tennessee

For information about this title or to order other books and/or electronic media, contact the publisher:

Hkamia Press
heatherream.com

Cover and interior design by The Book Cover Whisperer: OpenBookDesign.biz

Special thanks to Rebekah Burchfield and Tim Sowers.

Photo Credit page 147: Doyle Sowers

Publisher's Cataloging-in-Publication Data
Names: Ream, Heather, author.
Title: Fatulous : a memoir / Heather Ream.
Description: Knoxville, TN: Hkamia Press, 2025.
Identifiers: ISBN: 979-8-9882357-2-9 (paperback) | 979-8-9882357-3-6 (ebook) Subjects: LCSH Ream, Heather. | Overweight women--United States--Biography. | Overweight persons--United States--Biography. | Body weight--Psychological aspects. | Poor--United States--Biography. | | Poor children--United States--Biography. | Self-realization in women. | BISAC BIOGRAPHY & AUTOBIOGRAPHY / Memoir
Classification: LCC RC628 .R43 2025 | DDC 362.1/96398/0092—dc23 Library of Congress Control Number: 2025905172

979-8-9882357-2-9 Paperback
979-8-9882357-3-6 eBook

Printed in the United States of America

FIRST EDITION

In memory of Auntie Lois

Poet, Artist, Teacher

I love you always

CONTENTS

DOWN IN THE VALLEY

If I heard "Rocky Top" again, I knew I'd go crazy. I'd been at the University of Tennessee for twenty weeks, but it felt more like twenty years. I trudged up the endless slope of Cumberland Avenue that ran parallel with The Hill, a group of ornate and stately classrooms rich with history and the oldest on campus. The sun had barely crested the sky on this January morning, and it was too cold to do anything but snore blissfully under a cozy pile of blankets.

My psychology class was at the very top, behind Ayers Hall. The only way to reach my destination was to climb two flights of stairs and a steep slope. This presented no problem for most students, but most students weren't fat and asthmatic, unlike me.

I cursed the steep topography of downtown Knoxville. There was nothing more humiliating than panting with exertion while a dozen slender peers waited on me to reach the top of the stairwell. I slowed my gait and prepared for my usual subterfuge.

Before I mounted the stairs, I casually stepped off the sidewalk and unzipped my backpack, pretending to look for something. I tried to catch my breath. A flurry of students jogged effortlessly up the steps as I rearranged the pens in the bottom of my bag. The damp winter air energized them in a way I would never experience. Frosty temps only made them walk faster, the wind pistoning them past me like assembly line frozen confections. I rolled my eyes in disgust, partially at them but mostly at myself.

I hated the cold, and I envied their quick pace. Even if I walked as fast as possible, I would still be the last to get to class, and my only reward would be a hearty puff off my inhaler. Not for the first time, my heart cramped with longing as I imagined attending a more fitting college far away from my hometown – perhaps one built on a flat surface near the site of an abandoned shopping mall, or a rehabilitation facility intended for the ailing elderly.

My breathing eventually returned to normal, and I slowly ascended the stairs. At the top of the first flight, I stepped to the right as far as I could to let the students behind me pass. I did the same at the top of the second flight. I tried to take comfort in the fact that I was only one of 15,000 students on campus. Maybe nobody would remember my face and brand me forever as The Fat Girl Who Moo-ved Too Slowly. At least, not until I made my much-desired debut on the Clarence Brown stage — if that ever happened.

Five more minutes to go, I told myself as I braced for the last curved slope. I purposely kept my eyes on my shoes in an effort to trick my brain into thinking I wasn't climbing a hill. My eardrums and heart began to pulse in unison soon after. This was a futile gesture. Even if I managed to trick my brain, there was no tricking my lungs. Or my back. I wanted to swear out loud, fruitily and at full volume, but didn't. I needed all my oxygen.

Finally, I made it to my classroom. I once again paused in the hallway to catch my breath. A nearby radiator hissed as I unbuttoned my black wool coat and fished my inhaler out of my backpack. My chest had tightened with the first whiff of the dusty, dry air in the old building. I took a puff off my inhaler gratefully.

I settled into a chair at the back of the auditorium-style room and flipped the desk's top down onto my lap. A bit of the front of my stomach, the part I called my *baguette*, encroached the bottom of my notebook. I hated my *baguette*. It turned what should have been the slenderest part of my waist into an inflatable pool ring – an immutable, mushy reminder of my lack of self-confidence and muscle tone. I sighed and sat up as straight as I could in the hard chair to give myself more room. Sitting straight temporarily solved the *baguette* problem but left my back tense and tight.

A paralyzing thought popped into my head. I was only a freshman, and this was only the first week of my second semester. I would have to endure years of cold mornings, humid afternoons, and countless puffs of asthma medicine to get a degree. Plus, our family had been poor my whole life. Even the Pell Grants and scholarships I'd received wouldn't propel me into the middle class by themselves. Could I even afford college if the long hikes up The Hill didn't finish me first?

I wished I had someone to talk to. I longed for my best friend Davy and the rest of the theatre weirdos from high school. But we had lost touch quickly, and Davy's new chapter had begun at a different school. He was the one I missed most.

Depression enveloped me. It fell on me squarely, like a lumbering stranger on a plane snoring against my shoulder mid-flight.

Heavy, annoying, *inevitable*.

Twenty weeks down, one hundred and thirty-five to go.

~

I THRIVED IN HIGH school, despite our family's poverty. I had fallen in love with theatre as a sophomore, emoted a handful of lines as a junior, tackled Shakespeare as a senior. Despite my thick Appalachian accent and utterly Rubenesque body,

I was praised often enough by my acting teacher to think I might be talented.

I was no slouch in the academic category, either. I'd graduated eighth in our class and wore the coveted (by nerds, anyway) National Honor Society sash at my 1996 commencement, still managing to pull down a decent grade point average even as everyday survival stole most of my energy.

My biggest problem had always been money. Always. I grew up in a series of cramped apartments and housing projects. I knew the sharp indignity of accepting free school lunch and the tangy taste of government cheese. We moved into the fanciest place we'd ever lived, a trailer, after Daddy died, but over the years it had devolved into a shabby and dingy box.

Mom slung square pizza and industrial fruit cocktail as a lunchlady at Karns High, my adolescent alma mater, and my sister was a freshman there. I commuted to college — I couldn't afford the dorms — and spent my free time with my nose buried in a library book or pillow.

Mom, Sissy, and I shared the trailer with Cookie, our rescue hound mix whose favorite pastimes included eating people food and gnawing endlessly on her back. Neither Cookie nor I ever experienced satiety or a prescription cream for eczema, but the need for both was great.

Had I been born with a silver spoon in my mouth, or at

least, not a plastic one, I would have matriculated elsewhere. How I could have thrived far away from the calf-cramping, rolling green mountains of East Tennessee! I liked to picture myself attending a hallowed institution along the East Coast – a witchy, creative all-girls' college where we staged multiple versions of *Lysistrata* and cast spells of impotence on the patriarchy after rehearsal, in addition to the ivy-covered campus being flat and level. Instead, I picked the only school we could afford, the one in my hilly, unmanicured backyard. I applied to the University of Tennessee and was accepted.

Money-wise, my first semester had gone better than expected. After the Pell Grant and a small scholarship or two were applied against my account, the University wrote me a check for the leftover amount, which could be used for any kind of expenses related to college.

Our family had survived some very lean years, but overall, things were better than they'd been in a long time. Nothing crucial had fallen apart in our trailer recently. The air conditioning was still busted, true, but we'd installed a couple of window units, and they worked fine during the hot summer. Mom's Chapter 13 bankruptcy, the kind where one remitted one's bills to a scowling and judgmental trustee every month, had finally been paid off as well. We were reasonably healthy, too, in the same way a patched-up boxer with one closed eye might be as he climbed back inside the ring — battered but still able to withstand a few more punches to the liver.

Mom had been able to finance a new teal Chevrolet Corsica, and in gratitude for keeping myself felony and pregnancy-free, she gifted me our old family car. I inherited a formerly stylish, barely operational 1987 Mercury Topaz with a broken cassette player and a cloudy haze on the headlights, but it was more than adequate for my hour round-trip commute to campus.

Even though none of us ever had health insurance and my excess financial aid would have served me better earning interest in a bank account (or invested in eczema cream), Mom encouraged me to spend the whole amount as I saw fit.

The first-semester excess financial aid check was close to $1200. This was a jaw-dropping amount of money. I never had so much money to call my own. My after-school jobs' paychecks had always been shared with the household, and the decadence of the family's income tax return sprees never lasted long. As for Christmas – forget it. We'd been the recipients of charitable food boxes and Angel Tree gifts as long as I could remember. Holiday gifts were for practicality and to assuage the guilt of megachurch congregations, not indulgence.

I delayed the hedonistic frenzy of spending only long enough to open a bank account. Instead of cashing the check at Kroger like I'd done with my jobs in high school, I responsibly trekked my size-22 self down to First Tennessee's branch on campus and deposited it. Then, I spent every penny of the $1200 with great satisfaction.

I bought clothes – things like quality blue jeans from Lane Bryant that were reinforced in the inner thigh area (not the fabric-deficient ones from the skinny girl store) and trendy plaid baby doll dresses from Fashion Bug. Underpants that didn't have *Hanes* printed on the waistband. Bras that didn't leave me jiggling like a jogger when I was only strolling. A fabulous black coat with structured shoulders and a flared bottom that could have hung in Joan Crawford's closet.

I went to Metz and Kershner, a fancy Knoxville salon, and had my waist-length chestnut hair cut into a stylish chin-length bob that framed my face and made my double chin less noticeable.

I purchased a fifty-dollar tulle canopy netting at Pier One to cover my bed – my lumpy twin bed, which sat directly on the floor without rails or a headboard. In fact, all the rest of my furniture *combined* wasn't worth fifty dollars, but peering through the haze of the creamy fabric helped soften the nicked and balding carpet of my room.

And most foolishly, I treated my friends, family, and self to countless restaurant outings. Fancy meals were as rare to me as museum jewels, so I took this windfall as an opportunity to indulge my wildest culinary dreams. My choices were limited in a city the size of Knoxville, however, to sophisticated places like Darryl's, Red Lobster, or Chili's.

Chili's.

Chili's.

Surely I was the only person alive who thought the chef that dreamed up the southwestern eggroll recipe should be awarded a Michelin star. I had never once eaten anything like them at home, at my Mammaw's house, or in the school cafeteria. Those perfectly fried diagonals were as exotic to me as unagi sushi might have been to other Knoxvillians, ones who had traveled further than Washington, D.C. on an elementary school safety patrol trip.

For prom, Davy and I had eaten at an authentic French restaurant, made possible by a 2-for-1 coupon. I'd ordered lamb, which I was mostly unfamiliar with, and hard, saucy red potatoes that tasted vaguely of mint. The anticipation of eating at a fancy French restaurant made me dizzy with excitement, but I left disappointed.

I vowed not to make the same mistake twice, especially with my own money. I loved Chili's for both their exotic nature and economy, and I made no apologies.

Spending the excess financial aid was addictive, and I wanted more. Midway through the first semester, I applied for two credit cards via no-postage-needed forms fished out of my UT bookstore shopping bag. I had no job and no income, but I did have a valid social security number and the fevered arrogance of an 18-year-old ignoramus who was technically an adult. Between the Visa and the Discover, I was bestowed a $1500 limit — perfect to tide me over in case I needed another Chili's fix before then. Financially, things were pretty good.

On the other hand, I ended up flunking Biology by showing up ninety minutes after my scheduled final exam. I was used to cruising through most classes with no trouble, adept at memorizing what I needed to know the night before and writing entertaining papers that kept teachers from drinking out of boredom.

But with Biology, I simply got the time wrong, and the final counted for a substantial portion of our grade. The failure was a devastating first for me.

I'd begged my professor to let me make up the exam, right there on the spot *because I was late, not unprepared*, but he told me no. A stupid ninety-minute mistake cost me a whole semester of work and put my scholarships at risk.

I walked back to my car in a daze after it happened, shocked into despair.

Maybe I should have looked more carefully at my planner.

Maybe I should have transferred my exam schedule directly into my planner instead of leaving it on a separate piece of paper.

Maybe I should have done more than just glance at the exam times and then tried to rely on my memory.

My racing mind suddenly flashed back to the moment I'd received my exam schedule, and I remembered what really happened. I doubled over in realization.

I had shoved the exam schedule into my backpack after receiving it and never looked at it again. In a way, it was a miracle I only missed the exam by ninety minutes.

My intention had been to clean out my backpack and update my planner to regroup for finals, but I never got that far. Instead, I'd flung my backpack beside the piano bench at home, ignoring it as much as possible while I let myself be distracted by more interesting things.

The interesting things – pretty clothes, dinners out, plans for future credit card purchases – had deceptively loud voices, ones that muffled right thinking but also hushed my anxiety. When I tried on new outfits or signed my name on a receipt, my worries temporarily vanished. I wasn't poor or fat or lonely. I didn't worry about my future or if I would escape poverty for good. I existed only in the moment, my pleasure as remarkable and fleeting as a hastily chomped southwestern eggroll.

Had my feelings of inadequacy been quenchable, I would've been alarmed by the mountain of shopping bags that slowly accumulated on the piano bench at home in the last weeks of autumn, left there so I could savor the unwrapping of new things.

The bench had been covered for days by the time finals week arrived. No one in our house paid much attention to the piano except Sissy, but even she now eschewed it for her electric guitar. Mom, used to living with a couple of messy bohemian teenagers, also said nothing. Strangely, I had come to ignore the shopping bags as much as my backpack. As the semester had worn on, the thrill of shopping at the mall had worn off.

Glancing at the bags now filled me with anxiety and regret, so I tried not to look. I decided it was less painful to let my feelings suffocate under the precarious pile rather than try to make sense of them.

After a long cry in my car, I finally made it home. I sunk down into our itchy, worn couch and stared at the piano bench. My plan to deal with things later – any of the things — had flopped spectacularly. There was no need for misplaced indignation or excuses.

The truth was excruciating.

Oh, my God. This was nobody's fault but my own.

∿

I FLUNG MY ARM through the tangled canopy netting attached to my bed and slammed the snooze button of my alarm clock. I had completed the first week of the second semester mechanically and without joy. I did not want to get out of bed. The day would be frigid, and it would start with an embarrassing climb up The Hill.

Wait. Isn't today the 21st?

I wiped my eyes with the inside of my t-shirt and thought about it. It *was*.

Today was distribution day for excess financial aid. In a matter of hours, I could replenish my bank account. I'd have enough to pay off my credit card balances and head to Chili's again, if I wanted to.

I arrived on campus in plenty of time for my first class, but instead of climbing the stairs as usual, I continued straight on Cumberland until I arrived at the University Center. The walk to the UC was much easier, the sidewalk leveling out soon after I passed the staircases that led to the top of The Hill. Skipping class right after the start of the year wasn't a great idea, but I couldn't handle responsibility this morning. My first semester had felt like a total failure; it wasn't just Biology that made me feel that way. I also wasted a lot of money and didn't make any new friends. I hadn't really learned anything new, either, only how to navigate parking on campus and find the bursar's office.

My self-esteem was fragile and mercurial. Following praise, it sometimes bordered on delusional. Yet, no one had praised me for months, not even Mom. She was understanding but baffled over my first collegiate academic performance. Even though the rest of my grades had been good, they weren't enough to erase the squinched, worried scowl from her face.

Landing a role on the Clarence Brown stage now seemed laughable. I couldn't even get my debatably talented behind to a freshman psychology class. How could I handle the discipline of acting when I couldn't keep to a schedule? Every good thing I did in high school seemed a lifetime ago. At Karns, I might have considered myself a big fish in a little pond, but at UT, I was nothing more than a dead carp that had washed up on the banks of the Tennessee River. A *fat* dead carp.

My thoughts grew more sour with every step. A sharp puff of arctic air lifted my hair, and my jaw tightened with irritation. I was definitely too stressed to go to class.

I pulled open one of the University Center's heavy doors. The air inside was warm and still, comfortable even with students coming and going from several entrances. I waited in line at the snack bar to buy candy and a diet soda, hoping the cold would freeze off the calories from such an unhealthy breakfast. Distribution of the checks would begin in an hour, so after I paid, I curled up in an oversized cushioned chair and retrieved a paperback from my backpack.

When the hour was up, I got in line and waited for my check. The amount was the same, almost $1200, but this time I didn't feel the burst of excitement I did before. My stomach rose and fell gently, a coil of happiness kissed by an undercurrent of terror. Was this the feeling of adulthood?

I folded the envelope in half and stuck it in my wallet. My next class, the dreaded retake of Biology, was starting. All I had to do was walk into the auditorium behind me, pull out my notes from last semester, and barely pay attention until it was time for English Comp. I had done well in Biology, save for the final exam.

But I didn't. I turned away from the auditorium at the last moment and walked back outside. The wind immediately stung my face, but it fell to my back as I made my way to the car.

My legs swished eagerly under my jeans. I walked remarkably faster when I didn't have to scale the side of a mountain for higher education ... but was it just that? Something was propelling me forward.

What was I doing?

I didn't know. My heart was pounding almost as fast as it did when I climbed The Hill. A suffocating buzzing that seemed to emanate from the UC suddenly surged from behind. I had to outrun it. Well, outwalk it, anyway.

I just need a day off to focus, I chanted to myself over and over on my way down the slope, keeping time with my steps. *I just need a day.*

The buzzing had quieted by the time I passed the World's Fair Park and returned to my car. I slammed the driver's door shut and relished the relative warmth inside.

I busied myself with starting the engine and making plans to cash my check. Yet underneath the mundane thinking, the feeling of impending doom clung stubbornly. I tried to speak rationally to it, to myself, hoping I could convince it to leave.

Now, there's no need to panic. Taking a day off, even this early in the semester, won't ruin anything. If you'd woken up sick, you wouldn't give skipping class a second thought. Mom would have told you to stay home anyway. So, just pretend you're sick and go make the most of this day.

The doom considered what I said and finally loosened its grip.

I drove to the bank and deposited my check, vowing to skip the mall and go home instead. It was practically lunchtime, though, so it only made sense to stop by Chili's, the one next to West Town Mall, for takeout. Being mall-adjacent was nothing like being in the *actual* mall, and therefore, it was permissible.

Cookie greeted me with a furiously wagging tail and single-minded sniffs when I walked in the front door of our trailer. I turned the TV to the noon news and sat down on the couch with my lunch. Cookie, who usually ranked me third in terms of favorite humans, decided I was her new best friend and parked herself at my feet.

I reluctantly shared my southwestern eggrolls. Last semester, I would've deliriously bought Cookie an order of her own, but austerity needed to rule if I was going to pull myself out of this tailspin.

After lunch, I forced myself to empty the shopping bags on the piano bench. I hung a few new blouses in my closet and stacked a small mountain of new paperbacks against one of the walls. Once the piano bench was clear, I plucked the cordless phone from its base and called the automated numbers for my credit cards.

I gritted my teeth after hearing how much I owed but wrote checks for the balances. I was left with significantly less than first semester. That was ok, though. It *had* to be ok. My college career couldn't survive another F.

I was again smothered by a heavy plop of doom, and this time it brought along a feeling I'd known all my life: the hollow acceptance of poverty. I should have known better than to spend so much money. The path out of poverty – if you were lucky enough not to be felled by expensive illnesses or car repairs or rent increases — was nothing but an endless stair step of incrementally less terrible choices, a bittersweet gift made possible by scrimping every penny.

It took remarkable patience to make do with scraps of nothing, to whittle down your needs and wants to the leanest of sinew, the tiniest sips of water in the middle of a desert. And when better times did arrive, you had to be careful not to flood yourself with too much pleasure and security at once. If you did, the hard desert pan in your heart that made survival possible would be too dry to absorb enough to grow roots.

Mom and Sissy wouldn't be home for hours. They were in school, where they belonged. I went back into my bedroom. I parted the panels of the ivory tulle netting hanging above my mattress and climbed under the covers. I would catch up on missed assignments later. For now, I needed sleep. I closed my eyes and heard the jingle of Cookie's collar as she settled on the floor next to me. I heard nothing else until suppertime.

~

I RETURNED TO CAMPUS the next day and managed to attend my classes. In English Comp, I was missed, but only because group projects had been assigned.

I hated group projects.

After English Comp, I walked from the Humanities building to Hodges Library. I still had one class left, a basic college algebra course, but it wouldn't start for almost ninety minutes. Responsible students would have used that time to study, but I did not. I rode the library elevator up to the top floor and found a corner where I could be alone to read.

My chair faced a window that looked out on Volunteer Boulevard. The buildings of downtown Knoxville were visible in the distance. Downtown Knoxville had long been my favorite part of the city. Mama, Sissy, and I would take the bus there from the south side when I was a kid, mostly to window shop but sometimes to see Daddy at work at the radio station. He had been a good daddy. The emotional nuclear explosion from his death still burned, even after seven years.

From this cozy vantage point, downtown resembled a resin sculpture inside a snow globe. A gray, frosty sky traced the outlines of the buildings. I had walked every inch of downtown over the years, from the furthest edge of Clinch Avenue all the way down to South Central Street and the small Christian AM station where Daddy, formerly a pastor, had ended up a disc jockey. How I wished I could go back in time, if only for a little while.

The quiet library corner offered up a neutral silence, neither sympathetic nor hostile, only amplifying the voice that had been inside my heart since graduation.

I tried to blink through the tears in my eyes. Two escaped my lashes, falling simultaneously down my cheeks as I clapped my hand over my mouth to contain a sob. *How* was I going to survive this? Not only college, but what came next? Surely, the world didn't expect me to conquer adulthood after having been blown apart by poverty and grief.

I cried until I was lightheaded. I fished one of Daddy's old handkerchiefs from my backpack and gave my nose a satisfying honk. I felt calmer but numb.

After a while, the alarm on my watch beeped. Time to go.

I gathered my things and put on my coat. I walked back across campus, but instead of stopping at the Harris Building for my math class, I continued past it and went back to my car. Then, I drove home.

～

I DEVELOPED A NEW routine over the next few weeks. I would leave the house as usual, drive to campus, spend the morning reading and dozing in the library, grab fast food for lunch, and sneak home early, but not so early as to arouse suspicion from Mom if she happened to leave work sooner than expected. I never returned to class, yet I did not officially withdraw. In doing so, I guaranteed myself a full roster of failing grades at semester's end. I was unable to summon the strength to protect my academic history in this basic way. I did not understand why.

Depression blinded me. I felt completely overwhelmed, frozen by the thought of moving forward and desperately searching for the past. Surely I had to be missing something, or someone. Didn't I need time off to recover? Wasn't I supposed to have the tools I needed to build a life?

I had survived my childhood, even thrived – but I was still traumatized. I kept waiting for someone to swoop in lovingly, to hold my hand and gently encourage me until I was healed. No one had shown up consistently except the wretched doom.

I dreaded talking to Mom. She was also one of the walking wounded, having endured a dirt-poor childhood of her own and the early, sudden loss of her husband. She did an admirable job raising Sissy and me, all things considered, but it was clear that the greatest gift I could give was to become a fully functioning adult. I'd started out strong, but now I would add to her sorrow.

After leaving campus one cloudy day in February, I ordered a sack full of Krystal hamburgers and pulled behind Emery 5&10 on Chapman Highway. I parked my car on the side of the crumbled Big Lots parking lot that overlooked Duff Field, a position that dampened the constant sound of traffic coming from the highway. Chapman, perpetually lined with scruffy businesses and scruffier people, abutted the South Knoxville neighborhood that had been our home. I never felt too fat or out of place along its shabby corridor.

Krystal had been one of Daddy's favorites, too, although, perplexingly, he had been more of a fan of their chili than their sliders. Krystal's tiny hamburger sliders were ridiculously tasty, each one soft, steamed, and crowned with a single dill pickle chip and dot of tangy mustard. Their chili, however, was a murky brown nightmare that looked like it had been cooked in a cauldron.

Still, I ordered it sometimes just to feel close to Daddy.

I looked out over the overgrown remains of Duff Field, remembering happier times in South Knoxville, back when our family was poorer but still intact. I unpacked my lunch. I balanced a slider and my fries on one leg, near my knee, far enough away from my *baguette* so that nothing would topple over.

The first bite into the warm slider was heaven, but the feeling of bliss didn't last long. The sadness was still there, testing my gorge. Grief wasn't like a stomach bug. I couldn't purge it. It had settled into my bones. And doom couldn't be covered by a better outfit or anything else I'd bought trying to appease it.

The mental alchemy long used to eke out hope in the midst of poverty, of grief, of stinging rejection, had vanished like a desert mirage.

I whispered a prayer to Whoever was out there.

Please help me through this.

I yearned for a response. I heard only the sound of a drag-ster speeding down Chapman Highway. Maybe if I stayed here longer, or came back another day, I'd hear something eventually.

My second bite was tasteless. I swallowed it anyway. It was lunchtime, after all, even though I had no place to be.

BORN AGAIN

"You've been doing *what?*" Mom asked incredulously.

"I've ... I've been lying about going to class. I stopped going after the second week."

Spring break was supposed to be a time of relaxation, even for lunchladies. I'd just ruined it with my announcement. Mom took a long drag off her Basic 100. She was momentarily shocked into speechlessness, but I knew that wouldn't last long.

She kicked out the kitchen chair beside her and gestured toward the empty seat with the glowing end of her cigarette. I sat down. Her bright auburn hair, passed down from generations of redheads with similar tempers, shimmered through the smoke in the kitchen, reminding me of the markings of a dangerous tropical snake. I braced myself.

"Shit fire, Heather! Why in the world did you stop going to class?"

I wasn't sure where to start. Mom was my opposite in almost every way – brash, utterly fearless, and disinterested in acknowledging power structures, whether to dismantle them or climb their heights. However, she'd also proven time and time again that she was the type of parent you could call in the middle of the night when you were in a real jam.

I owed her the truth, but shame clung to me tightly.

"College sucks," I said, and burst into tears.

Mom ground the remainder of her cigarette into a thin metal fast-food ashtray that had somehow ended up at our house. It extinguished with a quiet hiss. Mom stood and wrapped her arms around the top of my head.

"Heather Pooh, what happened?"

I leaned into the safety of her abdomen and cried harder.

"Mama, it's so *hard*. I feel like nobody even knows I'm there. Or cares. I feel so overwhelmed by everything."

"Like what?"

"Like having to drive all the way over there and then walk everywhere. Plus, I haven't made any friends, and they gave me all that money and I'm still poor!" My voice stuttered on the last word, and it came out *pu-uh-or*, which sounded like the pronunciation of an ancient stage actress. I sobbed again. I would never have the guts to end up on stage, either.

"Why didn't you tell me?" Mom asked.

"Because I'm a fat failure who will never make anything of herself," I cried, humiliated to admit it.

"What have you been doing every day, then?"

I wiped my nose across the sleeve of the UT-branded t-shirt I'd bought from the school bookstore.

"Well, I leave the house and drive over to campus and hang out at the library. And then I'll get lunch and drive around for a while."

Mom's posture softened and she sat back down.

"Do you ever go over to Woodlawn, Pooh?"

Woodlawn was the South Knoxville cemetery where Daddy was buried. She had me dead to rights, like the time she'd busted me and some friends with a bottle of Olde English 800 I'd stashed in my closet. Sometimes, she was maddeningly uncanny.

"Yes. But that's not the worst part."

"Shit *fire*. You're not pregnant, are you?"

I sputtered with exasperation and scooted back into the chair. Classic Mom. Offer safety and then, just when I was most willing to share my vulnerability, say something so outrageously dumb it left a mark. I loved her a lot, but I wondered if Mom ever had conversations like this with my father, and if she did, was it possible he died on purpose to escape them?

"Oh my God. Of course not," I said, irritation temporarily shoving aside my shame. "The worst part is I stopped going to all my classes, but I didn't notify the school to drop them, either. That means I'm going to fail the whole semester."

"What happens next semester?"

"I have no idea. I doubt I'll get any scholarships. I might be able to keep my grants, though." The thought of hiking over to the bursar's office to beg for help left me nauseated. "Mom, I don't know what to do."

"Sounds like UT might be too big for you," she said succinctly, but the look in her eye was tender. She knew me. My parents had named me Heather, but a better name might have been Orchid. Conditions had to be perfect for me to thrive. In fact, I had been less a child and more a walking, exposed nerve ending, sensitive since birth and burdened with needs of special detergent and orthopedic shoes. Mom rode the bus with me every day of kindergarten because I was scared, then later volunteered in my elementary school clinic, close by in case I needed her.

I might have stayed in that protective little cocoon forever, but early lack forced me to sprout and survive in harsh conditions. I would never be a wildflower, able to happily bloom out of any old concrete crack.

"So, what if it is?" I asked flatly. "It's not like we can afford anyplace else."

Mom busied herself with the dishes. "Heather, I want you to finish college. You'll be the first in your daddy's family to graduate." Neither Daddy, nor his six brothers or sisters, nor any of my cousins had a college degree. Mom had earned a B.S. in Early Childhood Education, but it cost her the relationship with her own father. He kicked her out of his house when she insisted on a bigger life than her tiny Arkansan town could offer.

"I know," I said, ashamed. "I've always liked school. It's just that …" What I wanted to say was, *it's just that, as usual, I have to trade my wants for my needs, and after almost twenty years, I'm tired of it.* I didn't waste my breath. Mom was well-acquainted with the compulsory compromises of poverty. "It's just that … maybe I would really love school again if I had a choice of where to go."

"I always thought you'd do good at a little school like the one I went to," Mom offered, and a burst of anger exploded in my chest. "Yeah, well, me too," I said snippily. I'd applied for college on my own, with only Mom's good wishes to guide me. "But I don't know how to find one we can afford. That's how I ended up at UT in the first place."

Mom considered my words as she placed our forks and spoons, left over from the set she'd gotten as a newlywed, back in the drawer.

"Well, we'll just have to find one. You should talk to Ms. Houghton. I bet she could help." Ms. Houghton had been my high school acting teacher. She was a petite blonde with warm, friendly eyes and no trace of a Southern accent. I'd tried, and failed, to pattern my own speech after Ms. Houghton's slightly dour but sophisticated cadence.

I adored Ms. Houghton and had come to rely on her encouragement, even if I could never replicate her delicate pronunciation of the word "forehead." The word, which gently rolled out of her mouth as *forrid,* was in great contrast to the two enunciated shotgun blasts of twang that fell out of mine.

While I loved having an excuse to visit her, I knew I'd cry all over again when I told her what happened. However, Mom was right. Ms. Houghton could probably help. I only hoped she wouldn't judge me too harshly.

I decided I'd simply have to live with the feeling of constant embarrassment for a while. After hiding it for months, everyone in my life was going to know that I failed the first big test of adulthood. I had no other choice.

I tested Mom's promise of support. "Ok. I'll talk to her, but will you tell her about things first? Go find her at lunch, or something? It's already bad enough to come crawling back to my high school teacher. I don't want to have explain it all from scratch."

I knew if Mom agreed to tell Ms. Houghton, she'd also end up telling my former French teacher, half the lunchladies, and the principal's secretary. Mom was no good at discretion, although she never divulged anything maliciously. She merely had no filters – an open front door without a screen.

Policing Mom was like trying to contain a tornado. "Ok, Pooh. I'll talk to her," she promised.

I stood up to hug Mom. "Thank you," I said. Tears pricked my eyes again, but I felt better than I had in weeks.

"Things are going to be ok, honey," she replied and hugged me back.

~

I WAVED AT Ms. Houghton through the glass cutout of her classroom door, waiting for the school day to end. When the bell rang, I quickly ducked around the corner so her students wouldn't see me. I'd die on the spot if any of my younger friends recognized me. *It's a jungle out here, kids. Believe me, you're better off in high school.*

When the classroom was clear, I walked in. Ms. Houghton's eyes crinkled with a smile, and she held out her arms to greet me. I hugged her and caught the scent of her perfume, a woodsy floral mix that smelled expensive yet approachable.

"How are you doing, kiddo?"

"Peachy," I said sarcastically.

This wasn't the first time Ms. Houghton had counseled me. Twice during my senior year, once after a heartbreak and once after a fight with Mom, she listened to me cry and left me in such an uplifted state, I thought she might be an oracle.

"So, let's talk about it," she said, and we did. My tears made a brief appearance, but this time, they only played a supporting role. I was truly interested in her advice.

After an hour and two cans of iced tea purchased from the vending machine in the cafeteria, Ms. Houghton and I sat shoulder-to-shoulder looking through a catalog of colleges. I was open to attending a school outside of Tennessee, but not one too far away. I was already potentially embarking on a new adventure with the twin injuries of poverty and grief; I knew better than to get myself into a situation where Mom wasn't within a day's drive of my new home.

Surprisingly, Kentucky had several small liberal arts universities that fit the bill.

"What do you think about Kentucky?" asked Ms. Houghton.

"Their chicken can't be beat," I said, "plus, I love the Judds."

She looked at me in amusement as we weighed the pros and cons of each.

"What about Bellarmine? That's in Louisville. No Theatre program. Louisville is a cool little city, though."

"Forget it," I said. "No matter where I matriculate, I must emote beneath the proscenium arch."

"Noted. Centre College in Danville?"

"Last year, someone from Centre called to recruit me, and they woke me up from a really good nap. So, no."

Ms. Houghton, used to dealing with teenagers, said nothing but pinched the bridge of her nose, making her reading glasses stand at attention.

"Transylvania University?"

I'd swooned over Gary Oldman in *Dracula*. "Is that really the name?" She nodded. *"Drauch-yule,"* I said deeply, doing my best impression of him in the film. "Put it on the short list," I said grandly.

I was enjoying myself. Support from a woman I admired so greatly was invigorating. I felt like a withered plant being misted by a caring gardener.

"Here's a school in Williamsburg called Cumberland College. Nice campus. Theatre program."

Ms. Houghton handed the catalog to me. The pictures made the campus look pretty and compact. I read further.

"Oh, man. It's a Christian college, though."

"Do you not want to go to a Christian college?"

I didn't know how to answer that without spending the next week explaining myself. I'd grown up in church, the offspring of a former musical-prodigy-turned-pastor-turned-Christian-radio-announcer and a Baptist seminary attendee whose theological roles were limited because of her gender, or perhaps more specifically, her shapely bosom.

Baptist bosoms were somehow both a stumbling block to weaker brothers in Christ and the God-given gift that allowed women to attract husbands whose jobs it was to protect them from employment, leadership, and the stares of the weaker brethren.

Both Mama and Daddy eventually broke free of the Pharisaical church culture, but they still followed the teachings of Jesus. Daddy had been the gentlest Christian I'd ever known and had chosen quiet Bible study over formal worship. Mama simply found a different denomination after Daddy's death and left the Baptists behind.

All of us had been wounded by big Southern churches full of people who called themselves faithful believers. What many of them seemed to believe most faithfully was that we'd brought poverty upon ourselves, and they meted their charity thusly.

"To hell with those snooty Baptists," Mom said more than once. "Those pervy old deacons have been playing grab-ass with me since I was sixteen. And if it's not the deacons, it's the rich bitches in Sunday School class acting like they're better than us."

On paper, I was both an immersion Baptist and a sprinkled Methodist, but I hadn't set foot in a church in years. I still clung to a faith, of sorts. I prayed to God or Jesus or the Holy Spirit as I'd learned years ago. Mainstream Christianity taught that all three were separate but were somehow the same deity, which made zero sense to me. God the Father was like the CEO of the heavenly realms, and creator of all. Jesus, God's son who was also God, had been sent to Earth to live as a human and sacrifice himself to redeem humankind. The Holy Spirit, *also* God, was gifted to believers after Jesus was raised from the dead and ascended back into Heaven — an advocate, intercessor, and all-around supernatural mover and shaker to help us communicate better with CEO God.

The whole system sounded like an assignment in typing class. I was never sure whom I should address my formal entreaties to, or if "To Whom It May Concern," was adequate. All I knew was that out of the three of them, I liked Jesus best and prayed to Him the most. Jesus suffered the brunt of the abuse on Earth and raised all sorts of ruckus with the hypocritical religious folks of his time, in addition to healing sick people and performing miracles. He advertised easy yokes and unlimited forgiveness, two things I was desperate for.

Plus, the Bible taught that while he was fully God, he was fully human, too, and loved to spend time with people. I appreciated a deity who likely had bunions from years spent in sandals and inevitably laughed at fart jokes, because no one who traveled with twelve other dudes escaped without hearing a few rip on the way to Jerusalem.

Over the years, I developed a grudging respect. Our family had been rescued from random calamities enough times, it was only logical to believe in *something*. So, I still prayed sometimes, thinking of God with the same detached fondness I would reserve for a pen pal who lived in a different country.

As long as the three of them kept their distance — unless I really needed something — and I could sleep in on Sunday mornings without fear of burning in hell, I was content to call myself a believer.

"I don't necessarily mind," I said finally. "Depends on the Christians, I guess." Ms. Houghton nodded. "Do you know where Williamsburg is?" I asked.

"Cumberland looks close to Knoxville on their map," she said. The star marking Williamsburg extended over the Tennessee state line in the catalog's small drawing. The Kentucky border was only about an hour north of Knoxville. I knew this because one time Mom had missed her exit and accidentally drove across the state line looking for East Towne Mall, which was only twenty minutes from our trailer.

"Hmm. Well, maybe I should go check it out." I felt the misting of hope again. I scribbled the school's information on some scrap paper. "I should go. I've taken up enough of your time." I got up to leave. "Thank you. *So much.* I'll let you know how it goes."

She stood to hug me again. "You got it, toots."

As I drove home, I turned up the radio extra loud to drown out the anxiety trying to creep in. There were a million potential roadblocks between here and a return to college, but I didn't want to think of them now. I hoped the brightness of the day would glow long enough to illuminate the next step.

~

CUMBERLAND COLLEGE WAS SIXTY-NINE miles away from our trailer and a straight shot up Interstate 75. On the way, Mom insisted on playing her contemporary Christian cassette.

"What are you trying to do? Get me used to this kind of music so I won't roll my eyes so much in chapel? It won't work."

Mom had as many issues with organized religion as I did, but the community aspects of Christianity kept her happily planted in her small Methodist church.

"Be quiet, Punkinhead. I'm just praisin' the Lord," she replied, tapping out the beat of the words about an awesome God on the steering wheel, like a peppy Morse code designed to annoy me.

"Sorry," I said and kept quiet until we spotted the turn off for the college. We paused at the end of the exit ramp. To my left was a large gas station with a Wendy's and Baskin

Robbins attached to it, to my right, a handful of other fast-food places and a Walmart sign in the distance. I consulted the map.

This was the tiniest town I'd ever seen. "Well, other than the college, looks like that's about it for Williamsburg." Knoxville was no metropolis, but we did have two large stadiums and leftovers from a World's Fair. "They don't even have a Chili's," I said haughtily.

"You've got to check out the school at least, *Punkinhead*." Mom said wryly. I realized I was being ridiculous. Why was it so easy to lead with negativity? I was ready to jettison the whole idea before we even pulled into the driveway.

"You're right," I admitted.

We turned right, then left and passed a few normal-looking houses and a baseball field. The next right led us to Main Street. In front of us was a stately but simple large brick building with white columns. "The Baptist church," Mom announced, reading its name off the sign. "You know there's some pervoes in there," she muttered.

We drove down Main Street and made our way onto campus. Nearly every building, dorm and dining hall alike, matched the Baptist church. Everything was nestled relatively close together and set against a manicured courtyard crisscrossed with sidewalks.

"This place is cute as hell!" I exclaimed. I quickly pinched my lips together, hyper aware of my language in case God listened more attentively at Christian colleges.

Mom and I parked and made our way to something called the Perkins House, where we found the Admissions office. We picked up an application, and after a brief conversation with a kindly bouffant-headed secretary, headed to the Student Financial Center. Unlike at UT, the students at Cumberland weren't yet on spring break. I paid close attention as we walked, scrutinizing them from head to toe.

There seemed to be more girls than guys, mostly white, overwhelmingly dressed in unoffensive shorts, jeans, and plain t-shirts from Old Navy. Most of them were slender, but not all. I didn't feel especially out of place like I did at UT.

I watched a group of girls meet up to talk in front of the Boswell Campus Center, and a couple of guys who literally high-fived each other when they were close enough to touch.

"Straight out of a brochure," I said to myself in disbelief.

The vibe here seemed less rushed and happily wholesome. I mostly appreciated wholesomeness and tried to exude it, except for the times I hit my thumb with a hammer or ogled a shirtless jock running past me on Cumberland Avenue. How sensible everyone looked strolling along in their mid-priced sneakers and modest birthstone necklaces! The students at Cumberland weren't on the fast track to anywhere, except maybe Heaven.

Best of all, most of the campus was blessedly flat, as if it had been plopped in the middle of a crater. I sighed with satisfaction.

Mom and I soon stood at a teller's window inside the Student Financial Center. A pretty, middle-aged lady with untamed black hair counseled us on what aid was available.

"Your best bet's going to be student loans and work-study," she said, sliding the pricing sheet across the counter so I could see it. The cost for out-of-state tuition, room, board, and meals was so large, my heart palpitated.

"Give me that," said Mom, and took the paper for herself.

"Hell's bells!" she gasped. "Well, we all better pray the Lord makes it rain money, because that's the only way we can afford this."

Years of Mom's matter-of-fact public divulgences bare-ly humiliated me anymore, but I had to admit this one stung. At least we'd learned quickly that Cumberland wasn't a good fit.

The lady behind the counter remained positive. "Don't give up yet. At least apply for the loans and see if you're ap-proved," she said with a smile. "Work-study will make a big difference, too. What's your major? You might be able to tie your work-study in with that."

I didn't tell her that loan approval wasn't the only miracle I was hoping for. I'd have to be accepted as a student in the first place. A responsive reading I'd learned in church flitted into my mind. *Merciful God, hear our prayer.*

"Uh," I began, caught off guard by the question. "I don't know ... Communications, English ... maybe Theatre?"

"No kidding! My husband heads the Theatre Department. I know he'd love to have you for work-study."

Mom, a big fan of signs and wonders, perked up. "Did you hear her, Heather? This lady's husband runs the *whole theatre,* and you want to be on stage. Now, that's the Lord working right there."

Maybe so. It was an unusual coincidence. "What kind of work-study do you do for Theatre?" I asked. I hoped she'd suggest hanging posters with my name in the starring role on every campus bulletin board or schmoozing with big-name donors who'd write checks for each *Godspell* number I performed. Such high-visibility work would require an additional miracle, though. I could feel it in my soul.

"Building sets, mostly," she said, and I groaned inwardly. "Do you have experience?"

I'd painted a few flats in high school, but that was it. Tools intimidated me, even screwdrivers. I didn't volunteer this information. What was the adage? Fake it 'til you make it? I wondered how that would work if someone handed me a drill or something I could electrocute myself with.

I gave her my most wholesome smile. "I have some, yes," I answered with confidence, "and I'm a fast learner."

She acknowledged my answer with a nod. "A willingness to try is all he asks. You should check out the theatre," she said and gave us directions. "They're supposed to build a brand-new one eventually, but construction won't begin for a couple of years."

"Ok. Thanks for your help."

"Good luck. Hope to see you back."

I raised my hand in farewell. Mom and I left the Student Financial Center and walked to the large two-story building that held the theatre. Inside, the building smelled musty. I didn't mind. I associated it with childhood Sunday School classrooms, places where teachers tried their best to answer my never-ending questions and satisfy my never-ending requests for Ritz crackers and Hawaiian Punch.

We walked down a long hallway, and suddenly, the theatre popped into view.

All at once, I understood why the professor's wife had mentioned upcoming construction.

The theatre was ... unimpressive. Even shabby.

"Ugh," I said. "I'm not supposed to end up in a place like this until I'm an alcoholic has-been with no Tony Award® nominations."

There were maybe 150 seats, and stuffing hung out of half

of them. The carpet was a thin and industrial dookie brown that matched the color of the walls. The roofless sound booth was only accessible by a wooden ladder bolted to the plaster near the door. The ladder's rungs looked much too rickety to hold my full weight. Additional rooms were visible to the right side of the stage. I didn't feel safe exploring them, just in case a bunch of rats were rehearsing or sewing costumes like in a fairy tale.

"Honey, your high school was prettier than this," Mom said with a shake of her head.

"Yes, it was," I agreed, but I didn't turn to leave. Something was keeping me here. Maybe it was the honest tang of the fresh lumber stacked onstage or the semi-circle of unpainted canvas flats brimming with possibility.

A hundred and fifty people staring at me wasn't enough to bolster fame or infamy, but it also wasn't enough to give me stage fright. In fact, the theatre felt secure and intimate, an unintimidating space to connect with an audience.

A place where I might never feel overwhelmed or untalented.

"I can't believe it," I told Mom. "I *like* this crappy theatre."

"That's the Holy Spirit, Heather Pooh," Mom said solemnly. "You should listen to your intuition."

"Maybe." I replied. "If it is, Somebody up there's going to have to work this out. I don't trust my gut. My gut's the reason I ended up spending so much money on southwestern eggrolls."

"Let's go home and give it a shot," Mom shrugged. "You won't know if you don't try, baby."

On our way out of Williamsburg, we stopped at the Wendy's drive-thru attached to the truck stop. The cashier was my age, and she handed over our bacon cheeseburgers and fries with remarkable politeness.

Mom sized her up shrewdly. "Do you go to Cumberland, honey? You're so precious," she asked.

"Yes ma'am!" she answered sweetly. "I love it here. God put me in the exact right place."

Mom turned back toward me and smiled impishly. I fished two french fries out of the bag and shoved them at her mouth before she could say anything else.

~

AFTER A HUMILIATING TRIP to the University of Tennessee bursar's office a few weeks later, I sat perched on our saggy couch with the Cumberland College application in my lap. The bursar's visit had been productive. I found out that even with a failing semester, I could keep my Pell Grant. I'd also requested a copy of my transcripts to send to Cumberland.

I was informed that my transcripts would be released only after I repaid my excess financial aid from spring semester, since it had been awarded in expectation of class completion. I had nothing left with which to repay them. I slinked home in shame after my appointment to tell Mom what happened. She cussed for the rest of the evening, then took out a payday loan the next day, so I'd have the money.

Upon receipt, I looked at spring semester's grades only once and then immediately folded the paper into thirds. The transcripts were tangible proof of the worst parts of the past year. The subsequent act of applying to a school six times more expensive than UT was arguably skittering toward insanity, especially in the wake of Mom's new loan. Even *if* I was somehow accepted and somehow got enough money to attend, was I making the right decision? Poverty had reset my warning system in a way that blunted normal responses, and I was only truly reactionary to life-or-death situations. Everything else, except for the anxiety that led me to this point, was just medium terrifying. When your family was perpetually a few paychecks away from destitution, living on the edge felt as mundane as making a grocery list.

All I knew was that I liked Cumberland enough to want to go there.

Most of the application was easy, but I gritted my teeth when I got to the essay portion. I knew my acceptance would hinge on my response.

"Tell us why you chose Cumberland. Do you think God led you here?"

I wanted to be honest. Having spent years in church listening to heavily made-up soloists and flipping channels past shiny televangelists, though, I knew that many Christians also wanted a show. They wanted their honesty with *feeling*, praise Gawd.

I closed my eyes in brief prayer before I started my masterpiece.

Hey Jesus, long time, no talk. Sorry about that. If I'm supposed to go to Cumberland, please let this work out. I don't know what to do with the rest of my life. I'm so tired of trying to keep my head above water. Please let there be more, Lord. Let there be.

And let me razzle-dazzle these people. Amen.

I held nothing back, scribbling with so much force it left pen marks on the thick magazine on which I bore down. After I finished, I reread my essay and began to laugh.

The drama in my life – villainous poverty, academic success, failure, and an obvious need for redemption – mirrored a church youth skit so completely, I knew Cumberland was a perfect fit.

When my paperwork was finished, I took it to the post office with a renewed appreciation of faith and a burgeoning belief in God's sense of humor. Mom and I worked on financial aid over the next few weeks while we waited for a reply.

Finally, an envelope arrived, addressed to me.

"Mom!" I yelled across the trailer. "It's here!"

"I'm coming!" she yelled back, softly jogging into the living room, the backs of her slippers thumping her heels along the way.

I opened the envelope with trembling fingers. I unfolded the thick ivory paper inside, read it, and read it again.

"Well? What does it say?" Mom asked me, wide-eyed.

I was speechless. I handed her the letter.

The pressure of promissory notes, the realization of living in another state, the return of my temporarily displaced potential – those details could wait. For now, the only thing that mattered was the personalized greeting and the first sentence which read, "Congratulations on your acceptance, and welcome to Cumberland College."

MAGIC MAN

*E*ven though I'd be paying off student loans until I was eligible for Medicare, there was no doubt that Cumberland College was good for me. I made friends right away and jumped headfirst into theatre work-study, auditions, and classes. Williamsburg's slower pace and my instant success at school made the lonely days at UT seem like a distant dream.

People were nicer here than in Knoxville, which was a sacrilege to admit since there were just as many Christians per capita back home as there were in Kentucky. Maybe it was because the jerks were spread out more and not crammed into a multi-thousand-member megachurch like in larger cities. Whatever the reason, Kentucky folks were better. As a bonus, Mom and Sissy were relatively close by, so when I needed a home-cooked meal or a trip to the mall, I could hop on the highway and be at the trailer in an hour.

The only thing that bugged me – *really* bugged me – was the required code of conduct I'd signed in the Admissions office.

Premarital sex was out, and mandatory church service was in. Cursing was forbidden, even if the football team got creamed by an unranked Mormon homeschool group in overtime, and the non-coed dorm doors were locked precisely at midnight. And if a student was gay, forget it – their only choices were to pack a suitcase and leave or pretend to date someone saving themselves for DC Talk or Point of Grace, an impossible standard for physical intimacy that automatically imposed ironclad chastity and prevented awkward situations in parked cars.

During the application process, I agreed to Cumberland's rules unconcernedly and without care. Just like with the specifics of Christian doctrine, I didn't mind adhering to rules as long as they didn't cramp my style. Unfortunately, they proved harder to follow than expected.

To my relief, I found out that I wasn't the only one who'd signed the pledge with fingers crossed behind her back. My suitemates filled me in as we filed into the Rollins Center one morning before convocation. I steered us towards seats near the bottom, so I wouldn't have to climb any stairs, and listened in rapt attention.

"They let the boys get away with *everything*," said Danielle emphatically. Danielle was short, cute, and louder than an elderly mammaw's TV, which was not only part of her charm but also came in handy once the praise band started mic check. "One of the guys from Mahan Hall snuck his girl-friend into the dorm and they didn't find her for *weeks*. He only got busted when he snuck too many sandwiches out of the dining hall."

"Did they not kick him out?" I asked.

"Pfft. Are you kidding?" she replied. "They probably increased his athletic scholarship."

"Hey now," said Dylan, my roommate. Dylan was the coolest education major I knew – part preppy, part hippie, and totally easy-going - a personality that would ensure adoration from her future students.

"Girls get away with stuff, too. Do you know how many times the boyfriend and I snuck off to that gross little park in Williamsburg to ..."

Dr. Brume, my World History professor, walked in front of our seats on the way to his. We fell silent. Dylan smiled sweetly at him, her round Dutch Girl doll cheeks nearly eclipsing her eyes.

"... To clasp our hands in prayer and study the Bible until 2:00 a.m.?" she finished primly.

"Seventy times seven?" I quoted from scripture, and we cracked up.

"Ladies," Ana purred with a wiggle of her fingers, "do not forget my luscious Trinidadian."

The rest of us whooped enthusiastically. Ana was the most urbane of our group, majoring in pre-med and splitting time away from school between her family's homes in the Dominican Republic and New York City. "I've done some sneaking around of my own," she confided silkily.

Hearing their stories made me feel both better and worse about my behavior. I'd been boy-crazy since birth, managing to rope a few over the years but never hanging on long enough to brand them. The Lord tested my resolve in this area often, primarily depending on the weather and how often nearby sweaty boys lifted their shirts off flat abdomens to wipe their brows.

"Gosh, there are field parties where everyone goes to drink, and also that lounge in Lafollette where students go when they can't afford to drive all the way to Knoxville," added Carlene. "I'm lucky my friend Roy works at the security building. He's never ratted me out even when I sign in after midnight smellin' like a distillery."

Carlene, along with Dylan and Danielle, were native Kentuckians. Only Carlene had an accent that belonged in the movies. She sounded like a mixture of Loretta Lynn and a Scots-Irish time traveler and frosted each sentence with a healthy dollop of twang. Carlene could stretch one-syllable words longer than country store taffy machines, turning *Roy* into *Rowey* and *joy* into *joey*.

I made plenty of questionable decisions myself in high school, but depression and the fleeting pleasure of department store shopping had kept me from raising any Cain at UT. That didn't mean I wouldn't have participated if given the chance.

"I love that we're all secret hellions. I feel like a hypocrite, though. Does everyone break the rules here?" I wondered. "Why go to a Christian school at all?"

"I came for the good scholarship," Carlene said, "and my cousins went here, too. I think the faculty knows we all blow off steam from time to time. They only care about rule-breaking if the donors do."

"Huh," I huffed. Sadly, there was nothing shocking about Christian duplicity, but I had no right to throw stones. "I came here because I flunked my first year at UT and they took a chance on me. But I don't care if we have gay classmates or if someone is sliding into home instead of stopping on third base. We're all just trying to get through school."

"I don't care either," said Carlene.

"I also don't care," said Danielle.

"Me either," said Ana.

"I sure don't," said Dylan.

"Great," I replied. "It's official. Nobody cares."

The praise band started in earnest. Grudgingly, we rose

to our feet with the rest of the auditorium and began to clap along politely to the song.

"Yes, Lord!" they sang over and over. "Yes!"

Dylan turned to look at us. "Sounds like me at the park," she volunteered drolly.

~

I REALLY LIKED THE other acting students. We had so many classes together, it was easy to make friends. We were a mostly cheerful troupe who took our craft seriously, escaping the angst that often fell heavy on more experienced actors.

There was plenty of eye-candy at Cumberland, too, especially in our dingy little theatre. I considered three of my cohorts especially cute. The brunette drove his motorcycle all over campus but was also in the praise band, so he had the look of a bad boy but was as harmless as Zack Morris. The blonde, who was also my favorite acting partner, was long and lean with killer cheekbones, freakishly smart, and sweeter than summer strawberries.

But it was the pale-skinned, raven-haired goth boy, Aaron, who set my heart a-flutter. He hailed from a midwestern state even less exotic than Kentucky, and I found his all-black outfits and studded leather jewelry enormously intriguing. Goths were as rare in Knoxville as Democratic county commissioners. To study one up close was an extraordinary opportunity.

During acting class, I sometimes sat on my hands to keep them away from Aaron's short, glossy curls. His eyes were the same blue as a Tennessee spring sky at the height of dogwood season, and I longed to slather him with SPF 50 to protect his milky skin from the sun. I sometimes wished he was taller, to balance my width, but when I considered the probable neck pain from smooching such a Goliath, I conceded Aaron was better suited to my needs just as he was.

I learned to recognize the sound of Aaron's approach while building sets during work-study. When I heard the whisper of clanking chains against voluminous black pants, I knew he was nearby, and I would straighten my posture to thrust forward my impressive bosom. I didn't have much to say to him that wasn't related to lumber, yet to my credit, I never clumsily dropped a drill or dripping paintbrush trying to look cute and competent.

I did, however, once knock over a plastic bin full of screws, a gesture that might've even been considered suggestive — if only he'd been looking at the time.

Sadly, beneath the secret longings of crushdom was the rock-solid realization Aaron would never feel the same. He didn't have a girlfriend, but the girls he flirted with were petite and no-nonsense, fans of things like Depeche Mode and *X-Files*.

I was the complete opposite. Nonsense was an old friend, adding color to my life for as long as I could remember. Plus, I thought David Duchovny had the most punchable face on television and should be abducted by aliens to spare us his perpetual smirk.

And no one would *ever* consider me petite. Not in a million light years.

One evening, my dorm room phone rang. I was cleaning the suite's double sinks, preparing for our weekly Room Check. A few of Cumberland's rules made sense, and Room Check was one of them. At home, I only cleaned when threatened with eviction or disownment. To my surprise, mandatory sanitation helped regulate my mood. I discovered I enjoyed my living space much more when it was tidy, and especially when it was nicer than our trailer.

Dylan and I didn't have an answering machine, so I dropped the sponge I was using and hurriedly wiped my hands on my pajama bottoms to dry them before the phone stopped ringing. Thinking it was Sissy, I said hello with no pretense of formality, my own twangy accent dialed to ten.

"Is Heather there?" asked an unfamiliar male voice.

"This is Heather," I said, puzzled.

"Hey, this is Aaron," he said.

My breath hitched in surprise, and my heart began to thud excitedly.

"Hey, Aaron. What's up?"

"I was wondering if I could get your feedback on something. I'm working on a new show for a small club back home, and I'd really like to hear your opinion on it. Do you think we could meet up sometime?"

I twisted the phone away from my chin and mouthed *oh my God* to the ceiling. "Um ... sure. That's nice of you to think of me. When's a good time for you?" I replied, then cursed myself silently. *Idiot! Pretend you're busy and booked for the week. Don't make yourself so available.*

"What about Sunday night? No rehearsal, and it's after church or whatever." Rehearsals for *Twelfth Night*, in which we were both cast, ran only on weekdays. He didn't need to know I never went to church on Sunday, or did he? On Sundays, I preferred to sleep in and read fashion mags until lunchtime. Our required Monday convocation was plenty for me. Should I mention that? Not knowing his take on our school's Christian values only heightened my stress.

Maybe he's complementarian under that black eyeliner and doesn't like egalitarian girls, I thought frantically. *But if that's true, we're doomed from the start, anyway.*

I tried to sound carefree. "Well, I don't go to church on Sunday, but Sunday night works."

"Cool," he said. "I don't go, either, unless my parents are in town."

Another secret hellion, my mind whispered deliriously.

"Where do you want to meet? Do you want to come over to Asher and use the common room?" *Idiot!* I scolded myself again. *You should have let him suggest the place. What if he wanted to meet somewhere other than under the watchful eye of the Resident Assistant?*

"Sure," he said easily. "Is seven ok?"

"Sure."

"Cool. See you then," Aaron said and hung up.

"Dylan!" I hollered excitedly.

My roommate appeared in the doorway quickly, still holding the brush she had been using to scrub the tub. She looked at me curiously.

"That was *Aaron* on the phone. He wants to come over and show me some kind of local act he's doing. He said he wanted my *opinion*," I squealed happily.

"No way!" she laughed. "That's awesome. You've got the biggest crush on that guy."

"You bet I do. So, what do you think? Do you think he just wants my opinion, or do you think this is subterfuge to see if I'm interested in him?"

"Men are a mystery, girl," said Dylan wisely, "but if he's interested, you'll know sooner or later."

"I've got so much to plan," I told her. "For now, though, I need to work off this energy." I took the scrub brush from her and marched around the living area of our suite like a drum major.

"I'll finish scrubbing the tub," I said. "Hooray for Aaron's hotness!"

"Boy, you've got it bad," Dylan chuckled. "Enjoy your chores, weirdo."

~

I STOOD IN FRONT of the closet on Sunday evening trying to decide what to wear. Nothing looked good. My meeting with Aaron would be casual. Jeans were an easy pick, but most of my shirts hung sloppily to disguise my *baguette*.

I slipped on a blue-and-white button-up shirt, turning to the mirror to check my proportions. My *baguette* was covered, but the curve of my chest and waist was completely hidden, making me look about as sexy as a patient waiting for an x-ray. I cinched the back of the shirt to reveal my curves, but my *baguette* reappeared, upstaging my good parts.

A disgusted noise fell from my mouth. My *baguette* reminded me of the secret stomach alien from *Total Recall*, and it looked just as pretty.

"You need to shape up," I told myself in an Arnold Schwarzenegger voice.

Was Aaron standing in front of his mirror picking apart every flaw? I doubted it. Guys, even fat ones, charged through life with a confidence few women had. I knew one reason why women struggled with confidence — my room was strewn with glossy examples of it.

Women's magazines were great at balancing readers' self-esteem on a knife's edge. Each issue was as formulaic as an algebra problem, presenting a slender, undeniably beautiful actress or model smack dab in the middle of the cover and then lining the sides with recipes for decadent desserts and pleas to indulge in luxury shopping.

The editors created a reality that was *mostly* unattainable and unrealistic, expertly deluding us into believing we had everything in common with beauties like Ashley Judd or Salma Hayek or Halle Berry. We knew in our hearts that we would never look like them, but we bought the lie that we *almost* could, if only we purchased the clothes in which they posed or booked appointments for chunky highlights with their hairdressers.

My self-worth was held hostage every time I picked up one of these magazines, but I didn't know how to resist the strong messaging. I wanted to shove a candy bar in my mouth every time I saw beautiful clothes I'd never afford being modeled on a skinny body I'd never have. And yet, I kept buying the stupid things.

My neck began to itch from anxiety. I briefly scratched and to my dismay, small hives popped to the surface. I sighed heavily. An eczema flare was all I needed right now. Resolved, I reached for the only turtleneck in my closet, a maroon-and-gray hand-me-down from a church clothing drive that I'd owned for years.

The color blocking somewhat disguised my *baguette*, and the collar hid my blotchy neck, so I kept it on. I added faux pearl studs and a swipe of lipstick before squirting a dollop of hair gel into my palm to separate the bangs of my new pixie cut.

It was time to meet Aaron. I wiped the residue on my comforter and said bye to my suitemates, my heart pounding. I climbed the flight of stairs that took me to the lobby, trying to compose myself before rounding the corner.

Aaron was waiting for me, wearing jeans and an oversized dark gray sweater that complemented his creamy skin and blue eyes perfectly. *How am I going to survive this*, I asked myself.

"Hey," he said.

"Hey!" I answered loudly. I could feel my cheeks turning red. "Good to see you."

"Yeah, you, too." He gestured to his backpack. "Could we sit at a table?"

"Of course!" I led Aaron to a corner table, steering us as far away from the TV and the Resident Assistant as possible.

I sat, and Aaron sat across from me. He dropped his backpack beside him and reached over to unzip it.

"So, I have to say I'm intrigued. I've never had a friend perform in their own show before. That's awesome."

"Thanks," he said with a brief smile, still bent to the side.

"What kind of show is it? Like an open mic or something?" I could see Aaron doing a million different things on stage. Performing a monologue was the most likely choice, but I wouldn't be surprised if he had another swoon-worthy talent like playing the guitar or reciting original poetry to captivate any anemic goddesses sipping absinthe in the front row.

I hoped it was the guitar, though the thought was a fool's errand. Even a ukelele was too small to fit into his backpack. I allowed myself the briefest of fantasies anyway, imagining twirling in blue velvet peplum while Aaron loosed licks righteous enough to make Buddy Guy nod in approval. The thought of a goth with enough soul to play the blues made the heat from my cheeks travel south. I looked at Aaron expectantly.

"No, it's a magic show!" he said eagerly, slapping a deck of cards on the table.

"A magic show?" I repeated weakly. Magic was the most annoying onstage talent there was. It combined pointless jovial deception with required audience participation, and I abhorred the stupid *Ahhhh!* that was expected after the big reveal. Thanks to David Blaine, a popular new mentalist with star power, magic was making a comeback.

I wanted to saw him in half for it.

"Well, illusion, really," Aaron said. "Let me show you."

He spread the cards in a semi-circle, eyes tilted downwards. His long, inky lashes were irresistibly dark against his fair skin, and for a moment, I thought it might be enough to keep my fire for him burning forever, despite his revelation.

Then Aaron looked at me, azure eyes twinkling, and said, "Pick a card."

I was speechless. I plucked a card at random and silently watched his admittedly impressive trick.

After the cards, he performed several more tricks using props pulled from his backpack. I still couldn't tell if he was interested in me or not by the end of the routine. During his act, I'd made an agonizing decision. I knew girls often had to accept the idiosyncrasies of guys they liked (which was the only reason I'd ever watched Monty Python or listened to Pink Floyd), but this was a bridge too far.

The thought of watching the word "abracadabra" fall casually from such a beautiful mouth made my lusty heart twist with grief. I couldn't bear it.

Aaron was obviously passionate about his hobby. Magic made him happy. I had to respect that, even though I felt like punching a hole through a top hat. Although I hadn't really expected to end up with Aaron, I didn't think it would end *this* way.

I quickly grieved the years we'd never spend together as we made small talk afterwards. I would never see Aaron evolve from goth illusionist to house music DJ to weirdly hot Little League coach, but I knew my limits.

Once the props had been put away, Aaron slung his backpack over his shoulder and walked towards the door.

"Well, see you in rehearsal," he said pleasantly.

"Yeah," I replied. "See you."

Aaron skipped down the stairs of Asher Hall spritely, adorably pulling the sleeves of his sweater over his knuckles to keep them warm. I watched him until he was out of sight.

I returned to my room in a daze.

I tried to process all that had just happened. Aaron had offered no follow-up plans, so it was unlikely he was romantically interested. Even though I'd made up my mind that we had no future together, I still held out hope he'd be wildly attracted to me, making my decision harder.

Almost instantly, my brain served up a double helping of shame over my size, leaving me trembling with vulnerability. *Face it, Heather, you're too fat to be truly attractive. That's the real reason it would never work.* My chest tightened with misery. I was used to these poisoned meals, rotten bites of deficiency and self-disgust forced through my pursed lips and unwillingly swallowed. I ate them often because they were on the menu often – easy, greasy words always within reach and ready to stick to my ribs like elbows on a dirty tabletop.

I grabbed the stair rail to steady myself, gripping the smooth wooden cylinder hard to divert my thoughts.

Now wait just a damn minute, I replied with surprising force. *Aaron might not want to date me, but after that David Copperfield special up there, I don't want to date him, either.*

I waited for my brain to repeat its insult. Whether I had all the facts or not, I'd made a good point. I stood firmly but anxiously, wondering if I'd accept this logic or fall asleep later tearstained and clutching a cookie.

To my relief, I heard no retort. Aaron wasn't "the one," and it had nothing to do with my weight.

I stood outside our door for a few seconds to compose myself and then entered. My suitemates were watching a movie in one of the bedrooms.

"Hey girl!" yelled Dylan. "How did your thing go?"

I walked a few steps over and leaned against the doorway.

"It was magic," I told them.

They erupted happily, delighted for me.

"I'm so glad it was magical, my friend!" said Ana.

"No. His act — it was magic."

The girls fell silent, confused. Eventually, Danielle spoke

up. "You mean, he wanted your opinion on how to pull a rabbit out of a hat?"

"Pretty much. And that's all he wanted," I said with disappointment.

"What is wrong with that boy?" asked Carlene, her indignance adding an impossible third syllable to the word. "You're the coolest."

"Thanks, doll." I smiled at Carlene gratefully. "I don't know what's worse," I told them. "Being rejected or being rejected and having to watch card tricks, too."

Ana began to laugh. "I'm sorry it didn't work out," she said, "but it sounds like you dodged a bullet."

"You're right," I replied with a sigh. "I did. I could never date someone that into magic. Illusion. Whatever he calls it," I sputtered, "but I'm still going to have to see those beautiful blue eyes five days a week. How am I going to handle it? I still think he's cute."

My friends understood. They thought about it for a minute.

"The next time you see him, imagine him wearing a magician's cape to your wedding," suggested Danielle. "If you're not dying from embarrassment after that, we'll get you some professional help."

I stared at her. "I'm embarrassed *now*. Truly. Thanks for that."

Danielle winked one eye and made a fake pistol with her thumb and index finger. "Anytime, my dude."

It was time to go to sleep and try to reset from the emotional heartburn I'd experienced upstairs. "For my next trick, I will now disappear!" I announced with a flourish. "I'm going to bed."

"Good night, Marry Houdini."

"*Danielle*," the other girls groaned.

I brushed my teeth and lazily wiped my face with a washcloth. After I changed into my pajamas, I turned on a rerun and got into bed. One thing was certain – tonight's foray into dating had been a four-alarm dumpster fire, but I'd survived, and I'd learned something about myself, too.

Tomorrow would bring new opportunities for fun, maybe even for love ... one of these days. I hoped I'd have the courage to put myself out there again.

Single white female, curvier than a mountain road, ten times smarter than your most misogynistic relative and happy to prove it, seeks man with kind heart and incredible eyes for long-term relationship. Jesus stuff ok.

Was it really that simple? Could I, or my future love, condense ourselves down to a one-inch newspaper ad or proclamation on a truck stop bathroom wall? Based on what I'd learned about myself this evening, perhaps more detail was necessary. Some things really *were* deal-breakers.

No drugs, no ferrets, no disdain for hillbilly culture, no calling it "lunch meat" instead of "baloney."

The deal-breakers came faster and faster, numerous as colored handkerchiefs pulled from an illusionist's fist.

No funky toenails, no air-guitar, no proud belchers, no smug rock climbers, no book haters. And no magicians.

Exhausted but unexpectedly content, I gave my *baguette* a reassuring squeeze and drifted off to sleep, ready to dream of the perfect man. Or not.

KNOXVILLE FROM THE BUSHES

If someone was asked to describe Knoxville, my hometown, they might use words like "rundown," "average," or, if feeling generous, "adequate." However, if that same person was lashed to a rickety bar stool in a Maynardville Highway dive and forced to drink leftover cans of World's Fair beer, nothing but the unvarnished truth would pour from their lips.

"I've never seen so much litter," they might say. "The only thing trashier than Knoxville roads are nose-picking Vegas tourists with butt cleavage." Or perhaps, "Knoxville sports fans who root for the Vols are even more deranged than the people who see outlines of Jesus in their morning toast."

Or worst of all, they might ask the question that every soul who'd gazed upon our skyline had contemplated at one time or another.

"Is the Sunsphere supposed to look like a giant penis?"

Knoxville had its faults, but I still loved it. Almost as soon as I'd settled into the rhythms of my new Kentucky life, my hometown beckoned me back. It was strange. I certainly didn't want to leave Cumberland, but I couldn't deny that I missed the seasonal rituals back home.

Boomsday (known as Labor Day to everyone else) celebrated laborers' rights by shooting off a million fireworks from the Henley Street Bridge and packing the riverfront with corn dog booths, shirtless men with mullets, and crappy bands of yesteryear. Because of its white-trash flavor, Boomsday was a terrifically fun event, but also the event most likely to require an unscheduled tetanus shot. Attendance was a must, even though it was rough returning to work or school the next day sloshed, sunburned, and full of fried pickles.

The Dogwood Arts Festival, held in April, was infinitely classier. It was mostly because East Tennessee weather was fickle, and the early spring days were often too cold to go shirtless. Pastel pink and ivory dogwood blossoms would burst forth all over the city, and Knoxville would commemorate their beauty with a week-long event on Market Square.

As a kid, I'd adored the festival, enchanted by the local artisans, teen models, and glamorous clog dancers that filled every inch of the event space. Over the years, I was forced to relinquish my dreams of pageant stardom. I'd been too poor to ever clog my way up to the Miss America title, but I still possessed a soft spot for the dancers' sequined, saucer-shaped skirts and shiny suntan pantyhose.

Knoxville also had parades galore. Nothing fancy – just the usual high school marching bands and rumbly Shriners mini-cars. We loved watching them make their way down Gay Street every Easter, Christmas, and most holidays in between.

Sometimes, local celebrities would ride in convertibles along the parade route and gleefully toss candy into the crowd. Germ theory certainly had its place, but there was something special about eating a Tootsie Roll you'd picked off the street like an urchin in a Charles Dickens novel. Chewing the delicious cocoa mass and catching a whiff of sweat and gin from a former TV cowboy's hand was like eating a childhood memory. You had to be careful not to accidentally lick the wrapper, though, because it could kill you.

In fact, there were so many events I wanted to attend, I drove home almost every weekend to visit. As long as I didn't have rehearsal or an assignment due, spending two hours in the car was usually more interesting than spending Saturday in boring Williamsburg. No one stuck around the dorms unless they had to.

Predictably, Mom and Sissy began to tease me about it, insisting that I didn't live in Kentucky at all, but instead had set up camp in the shaggy holly bushes that lined the front of our trailer. I didn't mind. I liked spending time with my family, and there was enough separation between striking out on my own and landing softly at home that I wasn't overwhelmed by new ventures or restricted by familiarity.

Each festivity had its charm, but only football time in Tennessee turned Knoxville into a thirteen-week-long party town. Orange and white, the colors of the Vols, decorated nearly every business and home in the city. On game days, flags were flown, boats were loaded with beer and barbeque, and TVs were turned loud to announce the latest score.

Depending on who was asked, 1998 was either the year Tennessee would make history as National Champions or the year a hundred thousand Vol fans might commit seppuku if the new got damn quarterback couldn't keep his hands on the got damn ball long enough to throw it.

It was all very exciting.

Mom and Sissy weren't yet dressed for the day when I walked into the trailer that sunny October morning. The day was warm for fall, and I was clad appropriately in cotton leggings and my oversized UT tee shirt, left over from my failed matriculation there.

"I'm home!" I announced, flinging open the screen door.

Only Cookie paid any attention. She jumped off the couch in two parts, looking like a Slinky drawn on an Etch-a-Sketch.

"I just watered the bushes," deadpanned Mom. "I figured you'd come back inside so you wouldn't get rained on."

"Simply *hilarious*," I replied. "What do you guys want to do today?"

Mama and Sissy sighed in unison. I could feel their lack of enthusiasm from across the living room. "I'm taking Sissy over to Frances' house later to spend the night, so you'll just have me for entertainment," said Mom.

"Rats," I grumbled. Sissy was a lot of fun, especially now that she was in high school. I'd considered her my sidekick since birth, and it was hard getting used to the fact that she wasn't stuck at the house as much and thus not available to hang out.

"Well, excuse *me*, your majesty," Mom harumphed. "I'm sorry I'm not as cool as Sissy."

"You're cool, too," I hastily amended. I didn't want to shake that beehive. "So, what do you want to do today? Tennessee's playing Auburn. You want to watch the game?"

"We can't. We don't get the channel it's on."

"Rats," I repeated. "What else is there to do?"

"Lord, Punkinhead," Mom fussed. "This is supposed to be my day off. Let me finish my coffee first before you go planning your itinerary."

"Fine." I tossed my backpack onto the bare mattress in

my room. "I'll make up my bed while you get dressed. And maybe take Cookie for a walk."

"You do that," Mom said unhurriedly. "Just so you know, I'll be ready a lot faster if the dishes get washed, too."

I'd been outwitted. "*Fine*. But I draw the line at vacuuming."

~

WE DROVE SISSY TO Frances' house for the sleepover. Frances was waiting in the driveway, wearing an old leisure suit and a gray, bouffant wig. This was normal. Sissy and Frances, best friends since birth, had been producing movies on the family camcorder for years. The films' plot lines were nonsensical and the camera work dizzying to the point of nausea, but their finished works possessed a kind of John Waters-esque brilliance that was hard to deny.

Sissy got out of the car. Frances tossed her a ratty blonde wig, which Sissy caught like a fast ball. "Bye!" I yelled out the window. Frances bawked like a chicken in farewell.

"I never know what in the hell is going on with those two," said Mom as we drove away, "but at least they're not smoking dope."

"They're good eggs," I replied. "We're just a weird family."

"What do you want to do now?"

"Can we get lunch?"

"I'm broke, baby girl. All I can offer is a peanut butter sandwich or a bologna one."

Cookie, her front paws perched on the vinyl armrest between us, heard the menu and began to wag her tail.

"I've got some money left over from my work-study check this month. I'll pay."

"I'm fine with a sandwich," said Mom.

"Oh, come on. It's a beautiful day. Let's make an event out of it." Mom was right, of course, but an afternoon of carefree celebration was often enough to tide me over mentally for the whole week. None of us would ever get rich by choosing a peanut butter sandwich over an Extra Value Meal.

The standard advice from so-called financial experts was useless in families like ours. Frugality was already seared into our DNA. Occasionally, I preferred to dance in the shadow of the next unknown calamity instead, gleefully tossing any leftover fast-food French fries to the birds and not worrying about saving them for later.

"Why don't we ride out Central and go to Freezo?" I offered. "When's the last time you got an orange freeze?"

"Ok, Punkinhead," Mom said. "You win."

I tuned the radio to WIVK, smiling in victory. WIVK broadcast every UT game. Listening while we ate lunch would be a nice treat, even if we couldn't watch.

As we drove down Gay Street, John Ward, the beloved

announcer known as the Voice of the Vols, painted a detailed picture of Auburn's Jordan-Hare Stadium and every player therein. Ward's voice was pleasantly baritone but edged with urgency to whip up listeners' excitement. Fans hung on every word season after season, even though most years his frenzied descriptions called to mind the reporter who'd watched the Hindenburg disaster unfold rather than anything triumphant.

We *were* rooting for the Vols, after all.

There wasn't a soul on Gay Street, which was usual for the weekend. Market Square was a little busier, because of Watson's Department Store and the Mercury Theatre, but after 5pm on Friday, downtown Knoxville was Deadsville.

"Do you remember all the businesses that used to be on Gay Street in the '80s?" I asked Mom. "Revco, Woodruff's, JCPenney's. Now everything's boarded up. Looks like the backdrop of a horror movie about unfettered capitalism."

"Nobody wants to come downtown anymore, unless they work here," Mom lamented. "Ain't nothin' to do," she added.

"They've been trying to revitalize things for years. Maybe one day, it'll happen."

Mama was a staunch feminist, in her own way. "Maybe, but I'll probably be dead by then. It'll take forever to vote out all the dumbass men in charge."

From Central, we hung a left into Freezo's rocky parking

lot. Freezo was closer to a concession stand than a restaurant. The structure was barely bigger than a speedboat and had no bathrooms or indoor seating, but what it lacked in form, it made up for in flavor. They served hamburgers, hot dogs, ice cream, and the best chili and tamales I'd ever had, second only to Mammaw's.

Mom and I ordered burgers, fries, and orange freezes in honor of the Vols. Immediately upon our return to the car, Cookie hoisted herself onto the closed armrest between us, balancing on all fours like a circus elephant on a ball.

"Get your butt outta my face, dog," huffed Mom. She shoved the bag at me and scooped Cookie into her arms, repositioning her in the back seat. "You act like you don't eat better than we do sometimes. Heather, hide my hamburger."

I waited until Cookie settled and then passed Mom her food. We ate quietly for a minute, listening to the game. "You think this is the year we'll win it all?" I asked.

"Sure. Why not," said Mom flatly.

I knew that tone of voice. Mom used it when she really wanted something to happen, but experience had taught her not to get her hopes up. I'd picked up this habit, too, keeping joy at arm's length and never getting too attached to happiness. Disassociating was sometimes the only way to survive disappointment. Things stayed safer that way, but endless stoicism was tedious and ultimately, the choker of dreams.

Since moving to Kentucky, I'd glimpsed the possibility of leaving poverty and the endless grind of grief behind. I wanted nothing more than to infuse some of my naïve hope into Mama, to fête a future where we'd all turn out ok. With good jobs, Sissy and I would be able to buy all the orange freezes the Freezo could churn out, plus houses and insurance to boot. Who knew what lay ahead? On a beautiful afternoon like this, there were no obstructions, only goals.

"Stranger things *have* happened," I said, and took another sip of my freeze. The fragrant mix of creamy vanilla ice cream and tart orange soda made my taste buds pucker. "Delicious. Thanks for spending the day with me, by the way."

"Thanks for lunch," Mama replied. "You know, we're just teasing you about living in the bushes, Heather Pooh. You're always welcome to visit. It won't ever be fancy, but it's home."

"I know."

A burst of sound from the radio caught my attention. I turned up the volume.

"35, 30, 25, 20, 15, 10, 5, 4, 3, 2, 1!" exulted John Ward. "Give it to him. TOUCHDOWN!"

"We're barely into the first quarter and that's our second touchdown. Stranger things have happened," I reminded Mom.

"Well, if I'm wrong, next time I'll buy."

"Deal."

I finished my lunch in contentment, sharing with Cookie the leftover bites of my burger. Somehow, there was a scruffy magic around Knoxville that I didn't fully understand. No matter how hard I tried to pluck myself from its weed-ridden landscape, I returned as reliably as the Capistrano swallows. No matter what anyone else said, you could always come back home, even if you had to kick a few discarded Styrofoam cups out of your way to get there.

I hoped Knoxville would eventually live up to its potential the same way I might. Sure, some people thought us delusional, insisting on ourselves as the most beautiful and the most victorious, but there was no denying that things were looking up.

After all, a raggedy flower was still a flower, and the hardiest blooms grew best in native soil. Only gardeners with extensive local experience would ever recognize this promise of spring.

BLAST FROM THE PAST(OR)

*D*espite the fact my best friend Davy and I hung out almost every day from the middle of seventh grade to the last week of high school, I managed to keep secret a bombshell that threatened to blow apart our entire friendship.

I had been in love.

With him.

The feeling arrived all at once during our senior year; it took exactly one single sexy laugh and a brief scratch to his goatee to bring the realization to the forefront of my heart. Before that moment, later meticulously dissected in my journal, I'd considered Davy a comfortable and dependable part of my life, a part of our household the same way our cozy, threadbare loveseat was, essential but also taken for granted.

Afterwards, I *knew* Davy was the guy for me. It made so much sense – we were both children of poverty trying our best to escape. We loved the same music and movies. And even after five years of friendship, we still spent hours on the phone talking about any and every topic.

I had fallen in love with him during the autumn of 1995, and by spring of 1996, I was a dramatic, romantic sap, sure of my feelings but too terrified to say anything. To my great relief, Davy had taken me to prom, saving me from the humiliation of being the sad fat girl swaying by herself to Boyz II Men and watching the guy she was head-over-heels for with dance with someone else.

After graduation, the love-sick knots holding my heart in a chokehold gently began to unravel. My feelings for Davy changed back to ones of friendship. I still loved him dearly and thought him attractive, but I no longer spent my hours dreaming about our future together.

Adulthood beckoned, sometimes with an adventurous wink and sometimes like the creak of a haunted house door, and I knew it was time to forge past the comforts of home. I began to suspect that the painful waves of my romantic longing had been amplified — and possibly blown out of proportion — by our impending forays into maturity.

Graduation Day had been decidedly anti-climactic. During our senior year, Davy, myself, and several friends from acting class would often hang out after school or meet up over the weekends. We were perpetual customers – some might say squatters – at places like 11th Street Coffee House and the seldom-renovated Cedar Bluff Pizza Hut where our adorably goofy friend Randy worked. We partied in each other's houses and never missed the weekly midnight showing of *The Rocky Horror Picture Show* at Powell Theatre, the grimiest cinema in the county.

I started planning an after-hours hangout as soon as I threw my square cardboard cap up in the air. The minute our families grew bored of pinching our cheeks and crying over our accomplishments (and the looming cost of tuition), we could get together and have some real fun.

Sadly, my plans fizzled. I ended up at Denny's briefly with Randy and another friend, trying and failing to recapture the silly excitement of the past year. Rather than topping off the day with a special memory, I instead staggered back to my car, filled with an enormous amount of vanilla milkshake and a feeling of finality that made my soul ache as much as my stomach. That was the end of my high school career.

Davy started his college education elsewhere. We slowly and amicably drifted apart, staying in touch sporadically. Mom kept me updated because Davy had joined her small Methodist church. He'd left the community college he'd been attending when I'd been at the University of Tennessee. I was flabbergasted when I learned what else he'd been up to.

Davy was now enrolled at a local Bible college, studying to be a pastor.

As far as I was concerned, the words *Davy* and *pastor* went together like *peanut butter* and *lawnmowers*. He'd wanted to be a meteorologist as long as I'd known him, passionate about low-pressure systems and humidity indices the same way normal people were about their favorite singers or sports teams. I believed he would become a successful big-city weatherman ever since the Blizzard of '93, when he'd predicted the storm days before our local affiliates.

Unlike me, Davy had barely set foot in a church growing up, and while we'd stupidly gotten ourselves into a few risky (and sometimes illegal) undertakings over the years, inherent in my makeup was a mood-killing moral streak that prevented me from going too far. Davy was the opposite and went further every time. The idea of him eschewing his party-loving, dew-point-appreciating, funny guy personality for God was ludicrous.

And yet, according to Mom, Davy's conversion was genuine.

I'd unknowingly witnessed the genesis of said phenomenon. For my 18th birthday, Davy and several friends booked a room in a 2-star hotel that boasted a grossly warm indoor pool and an all-night restaurant. We'd stocked the shell-shaped sink with ice and the fruitiest Boone's Farm flavors available, celebrating my coming-of-age with foolishness and pre-emptive Tylenol to ward off hangovers.

Davy found the Gideon Bible in the room's nightstand drawer as we wound down for the evening and began to read it in between sips of Boone's and hard puffs on his Camel. Used to his quirks, I thought nothing of it at the time.

He stayed up all night reading it, skipping over all the boring begats but finding enough to hold his interest. Eventually, he started going to church with Mom. She encouraged him, answering his questions when she could and introducing him to other believers.

Then, somewhere between Boone's Farm and burgeoning faith, Davy decided that he wanted to be a preacher.

I couldn't believe it and told Mom so. I cycled through the stages usually reserved for grief — denial, anger, depression – but instead of being sad, I was incredulous. Faith was a great thing, and I was genuinely happy that Davy was experiencing spiritual growth.

But.

Except for my father, I'd never met a Southern pastor who'd gone fishing for Jesus but not fallen into the cesspool of sexism and homophobia that often dominated Christian leadership in these parts. I was fearful Davy would be pulled under like the rest of them, despite his unique personality and big heart. The Bible college he attended was reputed to be conservative to the point of oppression; there would be no fun, secret sin like at Cumberland.

I'd experienced enough mistreatment from organized religion. I knew the type of unyielding male leaders teaching Davy. They were long on brimstone and short on grace, rigid as steel beams and used to passing off man-made rules as love. One day, if Davy's plan succeeded, he'd be part of the same deeply flawed system that once hung a widow and her two children out to dry after the death of their loved one.

I decided I wanted no part of it. I returned fewer of Davy's phone calls and barely listened to Mom's frequent updates. It felt safer to let our friendship fade in the distance between Kentucky and Tennessee. Ironically, I thanked God that I'd never had the guts to share my romantic feelings back in high school. Now I understood the reason it would never have worked out.

Our paths had finally diverged. Life was taking us in different directions, but I would remain forever grateful for the good times, of which there were many.

~

DAVY WAS THE LAST thing on my mind when he called me that night after rehearsal. I'd been cast as Carr-Gomm in *The Elephant Man*, a role that Sir John Gielgud acted to perfection in the movie based on the play. I thought I was hot stuff. The head of the Theatre department, nicknamed Tex, could've cast me as the hysterical Nurse Sandwich or the boring Nurse Nora, but instead he promoted me to Hospital Administrator. This was the second time I'd played a traditionally male role at Cumberland, despite having plenty of guys to audition. My portrayal of Sir Toby Belch in *Twelfth Night* had been well-received, and I was confident my Carr-Gomm would be, as well.

I rehearsed my posh English accent on the walk back to the dorm. Preparing for a role was an exciting endeavor, and one I took seriously. I'd eliminated most of the natural twang from my impression, but my vowels still came out sounding like I needed an antihistamine. I had work to do.

Discovering the nuances of a character was such fun. It was part archaeology, part artistry, and a dash of alchemy. Carr-Gomm would no doubt be a stickler for order and propriety, torn between what was best for her hospital's public perception and best for John Merrick. I made a mental note to try to find a copy of *The Elephant Man* in Williamsburg so I could watch it and study Gielgud's interpretation as inspiration.

Rehearsal had run late, and it was close to nine when I got back to my room. Dylan was sitting on her bed, painting her toenails.

"Hey," she said. "Your friend Davy called, and he wants you to call him back. I wrote down the number."

"*Davy* called me?" I asked, bewildered. "When?"

"He called twice. Last time was ten minutes ago."

I hope everything is ok, I thought. *Oh Lord, maybe something happened to my mom at church.* I took the paper from the top of the desk. His number was the same. I quickly dialed the digits.

"Hello?" Davy said after a single ring.

"Um ... hey," I replied.

"Hey!" he said happily, like he was glad I'd called.

"What's up? Is everything ok?"

"Yeah, yeah. Everything's good. Hey, are you busy tonight? I really want to come up and see you."

Knoxville was an hour away, and my first class tomorrow started at 8:00 a.m.

"You wanna come up *now?* What for? It'll be ten before you even get here."

"I know, but I really need to talk to you. We could go grab something to eat."

The only things open in Williamsburg after ten were gas stations and Bibles.

"I mean ... if it's important, sure." I said with a heavy sigh. "But if you want to go to a restaurant, we'll have to drive to Corbin." Corbin was the next biggest town, about twenty minutes north of Williamsburg. The Shoney's in Corbin was open until midnight, a value-friendly refuge for anybody needing to refuel with a late-night shrimp platter and unlimited salad.

"That sounds good to me," Davy said. "Well, I'd better get going."

"Ok. Be safe. See you soon." I hung up the phone.

"Hey girl," I said to Dylan. "Davy's on his way up, and we're going to run up to Corbin. Will it bother you if I come in late?"

Dylan shook her head. "No, I'm good. Why is he coming up here?"

"I don't know. He said he had to talk to me about something important."

"Didn't you tell me he's a pastor now?"

"Studying to be one, yes."

My roommate giggled. "He might be coming up here to proselytize. He probably thinks God told him to save the soul of his childhood best friend, a lost, misguided jezebel who now goes to a heathen college that allows dancing and 'accidental' boob touching!" she proclaimed shrilly, tucking her hands under her chin in faux prayer and jostling the bottle of nail polish balanced on the comforter. "Seminary guys have to practice converting someone who really needs it."

"Hilarious," I replied sarcastically, "but if he pulls out a vial of holy water to throw on me, just know I'm going to act like I'm possessed by a demon with a smart mouth and a penchant for perversion. And the boob touching will not be accidental." I double-honked my own to emphasize the point.

⌇

EVEN A HEARTY GRILLED chicken salad and half a piece of Shoney's signature hot fudge cake couldn't revive my flagging energy. My eyes were getting heavier by the minute. I had listened to Davy talk non-stop on the way up to Corbin and all the way through dinner. I knew every detail of his conversion, his classes, and his decision to become a pastor.

After I'd asked a few questions to keep the conversation moving forward and nodded politely a few hundred times, it was finally time to leave. I still wasn't sure why Davy had sped to Kentucky just to tell me about his Intro to Preaching class. I was too tired to feel anything but vague confusion. I tried my best to keep up friendly banter on the ride back to the dorm, but all I wanted to do was sleep.

We were halfway back to Williamsburg when he spoke up.

"I have to tell you something," Davy said.

Something in his tone switched on an alarm inside of me, sweeping away the fatigue. What else could he possibly have to say? He'd talked all the way through dinner, completely changed from the person he was in high school. I felt like I'd spent the evening with someone from a different planet.

I turned to look at him. The soft roar of the wind from the cracked window was suddenly very loud. I waited.

"I think I'm in love with you," Davy said, the words spilling from his mouth in a rush.

My chest and stomach were immediately bathed in an uncomfortable heat, like I'd just stumbled off a roller coaster and needed to throw up in the bushes.

Oh no, I thought. *Oh no.*

There was a time when I would have given anything to hear those words. Now I felt nothing but a panicked clawing inside my mind. No one ever said life was fair, but the reality of requited love a few years too late seemed like an especially atrocious middle finger from the universe.

I had to say something. Anything.

"Wow. *Really?*" I answered cheerfully. "That's ... amazing," I said with a squeak, cringing on the inside. I sounded like a kindergarten teacher being handed a finger painting. I couldn't help it. I was stunned.

I tried to put myself in Davy's shoes. I'd almost been there a few years ago. I took a shaky breath, trying to appreciate the guts it took to reveal something so vulnerable. "When did this happen?" I asked.

"I guess I've known for a while," he said. "I can't stop thinking about you."

My stomach responded with another slosh of heat, this time with a flutter of excitement less unpleasant than before.

"I was convinced that I'd get into a wreck on my way up here and die in a fiery crash and not get a chance to tell you," Davy continued. He frantically ran his hand through his short, spiky hair. "Do you mind if I have a cigarette? I really need one."

"Sure," I said. My voice sounded very far away. There was a lot going on inside his Nissan Sentra, and it was making my head swim.

Davy rolled down his window completely, and the cool *whoosh* of the air from outside helped to steady me. He stuck a Camel in his mouth and flicked his lighter.

The spark of the flint matched an odd feeling building inside me. On the third try, a tall yellow flame finally appeared, and he quickly chased it before the wind could extinguish it.

The first puffs relaxed him into silence, giving me a chance to process all I'd heard.

My insides continued to simultaneously churn painfully and flutter pleasantly. Hearing Davy say he couldn't stop thinking about me was enormously flattering, even if he *would* be a judgmental pastor someday.

"Well," I said finally. "I'm very glad you made it up here safely."

Davy crushed the cigarette butt into the car's ashtray.

He was all business again. "So, what else do you think?" he asked pointedly.

Oh, what the hell, I said to myself. *You might as well even the score.*

"Truthfully, honey, I'm in shock," I answered. "I used to feel the same way about you."

"Really?" he said loudly, his voice cracking on the last syllable like it had in middle school. Then, on the heels of his reply, another question. "*Used* to?"

"I was in love with you our entire senior year. I never thought you'd feel the same way about me, so I never said anything. And after graduation, I thought maybe I'd invented the whole thing because I was sad about leaving high school. So, I let it go."

Davy stared straight ahead, clearly affected by what I'd said. He pressed his lips tight, hands unnecessarily twisting the steering wheel just to have something to do. "Look. I don't feel the same way I did at the prom or anything," I said. "You and I are such different people now ... but it's only fair that you know."

"Ok, that's it," he said. "We've got to go somewhere and talk about this before I accidentally drive us into the guard rail."

My watch beeped midnight as we pulled into the parking lot of Mapco, Williamsburg's only 24-hour truck stop. During the day, Cumberland students frequented the Wendy's and Baskin-Robbins inside the stop, but this time of night, the only refreshment available was gas-station java and utilitarian showers meant only for truckers.

We sat in an empty booth in front of the darkened Wendy's, both with large coffees. I was going to be exhausted tomorrow. I'd have to make room for a nap somewhere. I took a huge gulp from the disposable cup, grimacing at the taste of artificial French Vanilla.

"I really think you should give us a chance," said Davy. "Imagine going to our high school reunion and being together. Our friends would go crazy over it. Or your mom! What about your mom? She'd love it if we dated."

He wasn't *wrong,* exactly. Mom would be thrilled with anyone as long as they treated me well, weren't on probation, and worth eight figures, but I didn't elaborate. She did love Davy, and he had been a reliable friend to our family over the years. Maybe hoping he'd also be rich was a tad unrealistic.

"Honey, listen to me. You're very cute, and I'm sure you'd be a great boyfriend —"

"You think I'm cute, huh?" Davy interrupted flirtatiously.

"*Yes,*" I said with fake annoyance, "but I don't get the seminary stuff. I've got no problem with God, but fundamentalist Christianity sucks. Those people take out the humility and love and put in a bunch of rules and snobbery that probably has Jesus chugging the water He turned into wine," I finished in a huff.

Davy laughed heartily.

"Ok," he said, "but *I'm* not like that."

"Maybe not, but the seminary you go to is. And I'm sure your professors would just *love* to build a big, tacky cross and crucify some wide-eyed girl for wanting to be a pastor instead of a broodmare."

Davy laughed harder.

"I don't trust any of them," I grumbled.

Davy reached across the plastic table and placed his warm hand on top of mine.

"Heather, I don't have everything figured out yet, but give me a chance. I do know that I love you. I figured *that* out." His expressive brown eyes sought mine. I quickly looked down at the table. His earnestness was intense, as intimate as a state of undress.

I laid my hand on top of his and gave it a brief squeeze. Maybe I didn't have to have everything figured out right now, either.

"I never thought of you as the typical pastor's wife, anyway," he teased.

Nuclear heat detonated in my stomach, and I pulled my hands away from his.

"Pastor's wife?" I repeated loudly. I had about as much interest in being a pastor's wife as I did in becoming a taste tester for toilet bowl cleaners. "Are you on *drugs?*"

"For Pete's sake, I'm not proposing," Davy said. "Not yet. It's just ... something important to think about."

"So is world hunger!" I practically shouted. "Look, you know I'm cool with Jesus. But I cuss. And I like to sleep in on Sundays. And last week, I bought condoms for my friend Jennifer because she was afraid some Walmart employee would recognize her and snitch to the school. I'm afraid I've renounced my rule-following past for impious rebellion, my dear."

"What if someone snitched on *you?* They probably thought you were buying a box for yourself. You could have gotten into a lot of trouble."

I rolled my eyes. "Oh, please. I looked that cashier straight in the face. She wouldn't dare. Snitches get stitches, you know."

Davy shook his head as if to clear it.

"Back to the whole fundamentalist thing. Don't you think it's a tad hypocritical to accuse me of being terrible just because there are terrible people at my school? I mean, aren't you in the same position here at Cumberland? What if God put us in these places because He wants us to shake things up? We both went through a lot as kids. Maybe we're supposed to break the molds."

My mouth flew open like a landed fish.

"I ... you ..." I stuttered. I hated to be wrong more than anything, but he'd made an excellent point. Davy looked at me in victory, eyes half-lidded in amusement. He spread his arms across the back of the booth, quietly peacocking his success.

"*Dammit*," I told him. "I think you're right."

"I think you're beautiful."

I felt a blush rise to my face and climb to the tops of my ears. I realized Davy was telling the truth. He knew me far better than anyone I'd ever dated or drooled over, at least until recently. Because we'd been best friends, I'd dropped any notion of artifice or pretense with him long ago. There was no need to feel uncomfortable or unlovable around him, no need to obsess over my size or hide my *baguette*. He'd already fallen for me just as I was.

It was this monumental recognition that tipped me over the edge.

"Ok, let's try this," I said firmly.

Davy shot forward in the booth. "You mean dating?"

"Sure. Let's give it a whirl." He exhaled and scrubbed the top of his hair forward. The look of relief on his face was almost comical.

"I'm so excited!" He grinned and reached for my hands, but I slid them under the table.

"For now, though, you've got to take me back to the dorm before I fall asleep in this booth."

"Yes ma'am," he replied. We were back in front of Asher Hall within minutes. I'd have to sign in with the security guard since it was so late, and I was anxious to get inside. I needed to lie down and untangle my thoughts — or at least fall into unconsciousness and get some rest.

Davy kept the car idling as we said goodbye.

"Do you think you can come down this weekend?" he asked. "I want to take you on a real date."

"I think that would work," I replied, locking eyes with him.

"May I kiss you?"

In a romantic comedy, a kiss would have been the perfect ending to our evening. But I was no Julia Roberts, and Davy had been gifted the privilege of my unvarnished opinions long ago.

"Thank you, but it's been a weird night. If you try to kiss me now, I'm afraid I'll throw up in your mouth."

By some miracle, Davy managed to hold on to his desire for me.

He took my hand and pressed his lips to my fingertips. "I get it," he said. "I'll see you later, then."

Once I was back inside, I crept into my room as quietly as possible. Dylan was sleeping soundly, and I was glad. I didn't yet possess the ability to explain what had happened. I probably never would.

At least I hadn't barfed on my new boyfriend.

～

ON SATURDAY MORNING, I hopped in my creaky Mercury Topaz with an overnight bag and a box of cherry Pop Tarts. Since the car's tape player was broken and I couldn't tune to a decent radio station for another half-hour, I balanced my generic Walkman and a couple of tiny speakers in the driver's side dash so I could listen to music.

I tore the thin foil Pop Tart packaging open with my teeth and took a big bite of one. I was nervous and needed to get to Knoxville early before getting ready for my date. We were going to dinner and a movie, which we'd done a million times before, but the inevitable relinquishment of my most emotionally guarded parts afterwards – plus our first kiss, which I couldn't put off forever – would be a first. I was terrified and intrigued all at once.

Luckily, Mom and Sissy were home to distract me. I made it to our trailer park a little after ten and pulled into our driveway. The screen door opened with a squeal, and I heard the soft thumps of Cookie's paws as she padded down the sagging wooden steps to meet me.

I cut off the engine and cracked the driver's side door to pet her, enjoying the feel of her soft, pointy head. As I unloaded my bag from the trunk, Cookie took the opportunity to stretch her long hound body inside the car and grab the leftover crust from my Pop Tart.

"You scamp," I told her as I walked inside. She trotted in with only the slightest look of remorse. "Hey!" I announced in the doorway. "Your kid's home."

Mom was sitting on the couch, clad in a sweatsuit as usual. Feminine frippery bored her, and except for a housedress or two, she didn't own a single skirt. She had better things to do than wrestle with pantyhose or show off her gams to some looky-loo at the grocery store.

"Hey, woman, get in here!" she exclaimed, tossing aside the boxy cordless phone that was likely warm from Saturday morning catch-up calls with friends and family. I bent down for a hug. "Are you excited about your big date tonight?" she asked.

"Excited? Sure. Excited like I'm about to be pushed out of an airplane for skydiving."

"You know, you don't *have* to go," she said, looking at me knowingly, the way mothers had since the beginning of time.

"I already told Davy I was going to give this a shot, and I meant it," I replied firmly.

"Well, why don't Sissy and I take you out to breakfast to celebrate? Have you eaten?"

"Only a Pop-Tart, and I think Cookie stole the rest of the box." I was happy to have the diversion. I wanted to hear all the latest lunchlady gossip. I also wanted to see if Sissy had time to run to Big Lots with me, just in case they had any new weird, almost-expired snacks or beauty products priced for pennies on the dollar.

"You want to go to Shoney's and get the breakfast bar?"

Shoney's? Again? Even my diversion reminded me of Davy.

"I guess," I said.

"Well, c'mon, Punkinhead," Mom said, exhaling with effort as she stood up. "Let's go, then. And don't worry, Sissy and I both have plans this evening, in case you want to smooch Davy without an audience. Just don't go back to school pregnant."

I could have died. In an instant, she'd conjured an expectation of personal responsibility – a dour spectre wearing her face, perched immovably between Davy and me on the sofa like a stone gargoyle. The rules of her household were non-negotiable.

Mom was more effective than a chastity belt, and she knew it.

～

ONCE THE MOVIE WAS over, we headed back to the trailer to say goodnight. We'd had fun. We'd eaten dinner at a seafood place on Bearden Hill, both careful not to order anything too fishy or garlicky in case the Altoids tucked in my purse weren't up to the task. Afterwards, we watched the latest supernaturally tinged slasher at the mall. It was nothing that deserved a sequel, but I did find myself holding hands with Davy somewhere after the first victim, a snotty, rich-girl type who really had it coming, was hacked to bits.

Our conversation during the evening was light but heavy with expectation. I knew I looked good – Davy had confirmed that with a deep-throated *"Wow,"* that made my hours-long preening worth the trouble. By the time we were driving back to the trailer park, I was finally easing into the idea of us.

True to their word, neither Mom nor Sissy was at the trailer when we arrived. I unlocked the door and Cookie jumped off the couch, spinning in happy circles now that someone was home. Davy and I petted her until she was bored with sniffing the seafood leftovers clinging to our clothes.

Davy looked at me for a cue. I stared back awkwardly. I knew what I wanted to try next, but everything in our tiny trailer reminded me of Mom's gaze, as if she'd glued googly eyes to anything stationary. Davy took my hand.

"Do you want to go outside on the back deck?" he asked, and I nodded gratefully.

I opened the rear door of our trailer. To the right beyond our deck was the end of the trailer park property line, a nice, wooded area that belied the noisy train tracks to the left. Our backyard was a peaceful and private place, as long as the Norfolk Southern to Jacksonville didn't come thundering down the tracks like it usually did every five minutes.

The sky was black, softened by a scattering of stars. We listened as a chorus of buzzy things — frogs, late-to-the-party cicadas, or other creatures I'd never want to see in broad daylight – made their presence known. The evening was still warm enough to forgo jackets, but the air that moved over my neck was cool, perfect weather for Davy's arm to settle around my shoulder.

God, or Whoever was in charge, certainly seemed to be arranging a romantic setting.

Davy took my hand.

"May I kiss you now?" he asked softly.

The roller coaster in my stomach dipped dangerously towards nausea. *I promised him a chance,* I thought in dismay.

"Um, almost. I think I need a drink first," I babbled nervously.

"Do you actually *have* alcohol?" Mom wasn't a drinker, and Sissy was too young. Technically, I was, too, but found ways around it.

"We have the Goldschläger from last Thanksgiving.

I'll just take a quick shot," I replied. Goldschläger was a cinnamon-flavored schnapps with tiny real gold flakes scattered through the bottle. We'd ended up with it because I'd insisted we needed to offer an alcoholic beverage for our guests. Mom let me pick the brand, which was a mistake. I'd chosen Goldschläger because it looked beautiful, but every ounce ended up tasting like a gallon of cinnamon cough syrup left abandoned in the hot Texas sun. There was plenty left.

I walked back into the kitchen, leaving the door open for Davy to follow me, in case he also needed a shot of courage. I took the bottle from the cabinet above the stove, unscrewed the tinny gilt cap, and tipped the liquid only far enough to wet my lips. Our guests had learned last November not to gulp it.

The schnapps burned my throat as I swallowed, leaving a mildly pleasant aftertaste like I'd chewed an entire pack of Big Red gum. I repeated the process, dimly aware that in addition to having cold feet, I was also breaking yet another one of Cumberland's rules.

After a few more micro-sips, I felt calm enough to proceed and walked back outside to meet Davy. Cookie had taken advantage of the open door and was now sniffing in the woods beyond the deck.

"Are you ready?" Davy asked again.

"I think so," I answered, stepping close enough to feel

his body heat. I shut my eyes and leaned forward, only to hear the rapid scratch of Cookie's paws as she galloped up the stairs and over to us.

"Wait," I said to Davy, who had nearly closed the distance between the two of us.

"What?"

"I don't want the dog to watch us kiss."

He said nothing, but I recognized the slight annoyance in his exhalation. It was the same noise he made when he called Nissan to ask for a car payment extension and they put him on hold.

"Sorry," I said sheepishly, scooting Cookie back in the house with my foot and closing the door. We were alone once again.

This time, I didn't hesitate. I took Davy's face in my hands and kissed him softly. He wrapped his arms around me and kissed back. We stayed that way for a minute.

"That was nice," he whispered afterwards.

"It really was," I said in agreement. The kiss, if being evaluated on technical perfection alone, would have scored a ten. Davy folded his hand into mine, and we leaned against the deck railing in silence.

"You should probably cut out of here before Mom gets home. I had a lovely time, but our evening is none of her dang business."

"Good idea," Davy replied. I walked him to his car. "When are you driving back?"

I didn't have the emotional energy for another Shoney's date, and I'd already worn the only cute outfit I'd packed. "Probably in the morning," I lied lightly. "I've got homework to do."

"Ok. Call me when you get back to the dorm. Let me know you got home safely."

"Sure," I said. "And I'll come down again soon, and you can always drive up."

"I'll have to see your play, too," Davy added. "This will be fun. We'll make it work."

"Sure," I repeated, but my voice was drowned out by the car's motor. Davy reversed out of the driveway with his window down, waving bye with a cigarette in his hand. I returned to the back deck to let Cookie outside now that personal business had been concluded.

A gray plastic chair that had seen better days was pushed up against the corner of the deck. The chair was oddly flexible after repeated exposures to the elements. I sat down anyway.

My time with Davy had been wonderful, but I knew something was still missing. Technical perfection wasn't enough. Could I fall in love with Davy again, as he had fallen in love with me?

I thought I might already know the answer. I wasn't

ready to offer it up yet. There was comfort in having a cute boyfriend, even a long-distance one. With dating came a lottery-sized infusion of social currency that was rare for fat girls. There was nothing wrong with acknowledging this realization slowly, was there? What was the harm in putting a heart-shaped framed picture of him in my dorm room's windowsill, or introducing him to my fellow actors – especially the cute one who'd rejected me — after the show, or letting the phrase *my boyfriend* brightly dot my conversations like cherries atop sundaes? It wasn't a crime.

No law, not even the Ten Commandments, said I had to admit to myself what I already knew.

The many iterations of Davy flipped through my mind like a classroom filmstrip. Davy on the first day of eighth grade, wearing overalls with one strap undone and sporting a freshly pierced ear, assured of his coolness. Davy prank calling grocery stores and gas stations, sending hapless employees to the aisles to look for made-up products. Davy bringing over pizza after pizza from his job at Little Caesars, helping our family bridge the gaps between paychecks during the leanest years. Me, proudly entering the prom wearing a dress from Sears' clearance rack, Davy on my arm. Me, grateful to have known such a quirky, funny, precious soul – whether I was in love with him or not.

How wonderful it would be to return his feelings, to sink

with ease into a ready-made romance! There'd be no games, no drama over finances or navigating mothers' hurt feelings on holidays because our families were already so close. I'd never have to convince a man ever again that I was lovable, despite my size.

Reciprocity would solve so many of my problems.

And yet, I hesitated. Future Heather, the one whose hard-earned wisdom was whispering a warning to her college-aged self, had already slammed the emergency brake straight to the floor. Her voice drowned out all other thoughts.

She told me a story. In it, Davy stood behind a pulpit, resplendent in satin robes, preaching out of the Bible in a soothing voice. I listened to him while our toddler fidgeted sleepily on my lap, fighting the heaviness of her long-lashed eyelids.

To my right was our adolescent daughter, old enough to understand the responsibility of being the pastor's daughter but not yet burdened by it, sitting tall with good posture and eager to show off her good behavior. She kindly retrieved more paper and crayons out of my oversized purse for her other sister, a rumpled imp with a jack-o-lantern smile.

My family was beautiful, yet I couldn't summon a clear picture of my own face. I felt as though I was smiling, always smiling, a picture-perfect refuge for my children and my husband's congregation. Sadly, I knew my passions had faded; my love for acting devolved into directing endless

Vacation Bible School skits; my formerly filthy vocabulary replaced by worthless substitutions that did nothing to quell the emotion behind them. My clothes were modest and boring, easy-care fabric softly outlining the spent fibers of my breasts and abdomen.

I loved my babies unconditionally, but somehow, I knew I'd poured into them all that was left of myself, so much that the Heather contemplating her life on a shabby back deck had ceased to exist. She'd been pulled apart and fed into the eternal sacrificial machine of motherhood long ago.

Is this what you want? This ... silent sainthood?

For years, poverty rendered me invisible. Hopes and dreams had been a luxury, perpetually overshadowed by the need to survive. College, even with its ups and downs, was finally giving me a chance to shine. Maybe I'd be rich someday. Or famous. Maybe.

I wanted to regret nothing, but if Davy and I built a life together, I would regret many things — including the construction of our stifling shelter, the place where'd we'd broken ground tonight. Comfort, while enticing, cost too much. I didn't want to trade my imperfect potential for a perfectly comfortable future.

MY potential.

My heart began to thump quickly. I knew the answer. The world was too full of wonderous wildness to settle down almost as soon as I found my voice. I would find others who spoke my language, others to love me unconditionally. I just needed to be brave enough to believe it. I would need to be honest with Davy, but I thought I was brave enough to do that, too.

Now burdened and blessed with the gift of foresight, I defiantly leaned back in the wobbly chair as if to telegraph my intentions to the universe. I dared God to tell me I was wrong. I heard only the sounds of His creation.

Somewhere beyond the woods of our trailer park, adventure was waiting.

THE KINGDOM, AND THE POWER, AND THE DOLLY FOREVER

Commuting an hour each way to a daily summer job was inarguably stupid, unless that summer job happened to be at Dollywood. Before working there, I'd never considered myself a theme park person. Not only had I once ralphed spectacularly after a ride in a fake pirate ship, I also preferred to bypass any experience that risked my size-22 derrière getting stuck in a rigid roller coaster seat.

Dollywood was different, though. They had rides ranging from kiddy cars to rampaging river boats, but they balanced it with plenty of entertainment for the old and plump folks. Even if someone was scared to death of Daredevil Falls, they could still stand terrifyingly close to rehabilitated bald eagles or dip handmade candles in hot colored wax while "Baby I'm Burnin" played over rock-shaped outdoor speakers.

Plus, Mom, Sissy, and I adored Dolly Parton. She was

practically family. In addition to making East Tennessee proud in general, our great-aunt Irene, also an employee, had rubbed elbows with her plenty of times in the park, making her a blood relative by proxy. Most importantly, Dolly had grown up even poorer than us and managed to earn a bazillion dollars without becoming a stuck-up, big-city defender, creating the Dollywood empire and bringing dignified jobs to her small hometown.

There were only two people who walked on water as far as Mama and I were concerned, and one of them did it in hot pink heels.

Since lunchladies didn't get paid during school breaks, Mom was used to having a second, or third, job. In years past, she'd slung breakfast at McDonald's, cleaned hotel rooms for a pittance, and hoisted huge bags of mail at the post office, hoping to get hired on full-time. She was an authority on the worst careers available for the working class, so the fact that she would spend time, money, and effort on something temporary spoke not only to the quality of the job but also her sense of belonging.

All three of us worked in food service at Dollywood. We'd been hired on the spot after a brief glance at our résumés revealed a combined decade of experience. Dish room labor, pizza making, and Sunday waitressing for picky patrons (the bulk of whom were Christian, flush with the Holy Spirit but never cash for tips) weren't impressive careers, but at Dollywood, we were blessed and highly favored.

My supervisor had asked my preference on where to work in the park, or if I didn't have a preference, he would decide for me. I knew the importance of choosing for myself. Choice was a non-negotiable freedom in all aspects of a woman's life. It was *particularly* crucial when trying to determine one's potential for heat stroke.

If I'd let someone else pick, I might've ended up in Craftsman's Valley, where the female employees had to wear long calico dresses and beribboned caps no matter the time of year. I wasn't as strong as my ancestors. I couldn't bear a sweltering summer with only sweat to cool me off. Even the privilege of squatting over an electric fan all day, a prospect that would've had my mountain grandmothers sighing in relief, was inadequate for my easily overheated constitution.

I decided to spend my summer in Jukebox Junction, the section of Dollywood designed to look like Sevierville, TN in the 1950s. Jukebox Junction reminded me of Andy Griffith's Mayberry. Vintage pastel cars dotted the perimeter of a streetscape lined with faux storefronts for TVs, fashions, and furniture. Authentic commercials played between '50s songs on a soundtrack that was surprisingly rockin', even on repeat.

The uniform for Jukebox Junction was manageable. I wore

a white button-down shirt, jeans, and a jaunty polyester scarf I threaded through my collar. The wardrobe department had also offered a poodle skirt, in case the jeans were too warm, but I hadn't worn anything with a dog on it since I was a toddler, and I wasn't going to start again now.

The average working day for our family was long, often lasting from park open to close. Sometimes, when business was slow, a manager might close a stand early, giving whoever worked there the rest of the evening off. Of the three of us, this happened to me the most. Guests tended to leave the perimeters of the park as the evening wore on, often returning to the park's main drag, Showstreet, for the latest country revue and Dolly-related shopping.

Sissy, because of her unusual teenage competence, was given a Showstreet sausage stand to run. She hated her sausage stand with the heat of a thousand suns, which was also the approximate temperature inside the booth. Half the booth's square footage was occupied by a giant skillet, over which Sissy and her wilted auburn curls presided, grilling kielbasas and onions for delirious Northern tourists. These piteous creatures were clearly affected by malady, for nothing but the fever of dehydration would cause a perspiring man to cram a steaming hot sandwich in his mouth in the middle of July.

Sometimes after work, I'd hunker in the back of the sausage stand and hang out with Sissy. I admired her approach to these customers. Her tone was sweet, but tart, like the first bite of a Granny Smith apple. Sissy would repeat their order back to them, coolly and politely. Something in her tone would cause the customer to instinctively bristle at the unidentifiable but definite undercurrent of her words. They would retreat confusedly, immediately self-medicating with a bite of their sizzling hoagie in an attempt to deflect her masterly frostiness.

Sissy, who had the all the brains, beauty, and drive needed for world domination, may have been unable to stop them from patronizing her booth in the first place, but her honeyed intimidation guaranteed only the most masochistic would return. And weirdly, they did.

I hardly ever saw Mom. She worked the food line at Aunt Granny's, the park's only buffet. Because it was a sit-down restaurant, the employees consistently worked past closing. There was always a group of thoughtless tourists saddling up to the steam trays ten minutes before Dollywood shut down for the night. Aunt Granny's was hard work, and when I did get a chance to see Mom, she didn't have time to talk and was usually stinking of an unholy mix of bleach water and fried chicken.

I had the best food service job at Dollywood, hands down. Most days, I was alone in an air-conditioned square box painted to look like Jukebox Junction's telephone company.

I made and sold pretzels. The only reason my booth was air-conditioned was because I worked with raw dough, but once I opened the front hatch on the *Tennessee Telephone* each morning, the heavy humidity of summer replaced the icy cool within minutes. Still, it was a pleasant location. Soft pretzels were tasty. When matched against the adorable Red's Diner next door, however, most people flocked to their more traditional '50s menu.

I rolled out pretzels a few times a day, but the bulk of my business was selling soda. The rest of the time, I wrote postcards to friends and surreptitiously read Stephen King paperbacks. I was well aware that this was one of the last summers before the responsibilities of adult productivity smothered me, with no relief and no parole until retirement. I intended to enjoy every minute.

I stood in my booth late one afternoon, bopping along mindlessly to a zany song about tan shoes and pink shoelaces. I was making a list of things I'd need to pack to take back to the dorm in a few weeks. The summer had flown by, and I was excited about my return to Kentucky. A lot had happened.

After nine agonizing months, Davy and I had broken up. I'd known from the start we'd never last. I'd ignored my intuition anyway just to have a fun and cute companion at the ready. My body rebelled for disregarding its wisdom, and I'd been anxious and itchier than normal since last autumn.

I'd officially ended things after Davy blew off a Saturday evening with me to fill water balloons for a youth group meeting, yet it was fair to say the breakup was mutual. We'd had a good time, but ultimately, the spark wasn't there. I was bad about trying to outrun emotional pain, using every available tool of deflection to postpone the task of processing my feelings. However, delaying the inevitable had been unfair to both of us.

I tried to recapture my high school feelings and fall back in love. I really did, but I found nothing but effort and frustration in time-travel.

My brief recollection of the events caused a twitch in my scalp that knocked the diamanté cat-eye sunglasses off my head. They landed on my nose with a painful thump. One thing I knew for sure: I deserved to love and be loved by someone well-suited for me, and the sooner, the better. Anytime God felt like sending him along would be swell.

"Twilight Time" by The Platters replaced the cheerful hiccups of Dodie Stevens, and I took a moment to appreciate the backlot-like quality of my surroundings. Wandering around Dollywood, especially after the park had closed, was like sneaking onto a movie set in the middle of the night. Reality and rose-colored remembrance blended in every corner, from the lye soap makers just south of the Blazing Fury to the living sock-hop of Jukebox Junction. I was as embarrassingly susceptible to the wistful nostalgia as much as any guest was — maybe more so, since I knew by virtue of my blue-collar birth that if born for real in The Olden Days, I'd have starved to death or died of consumption years before adolescence. To me, the park was a laudanum-soaked handkerchief, always ready to lure folks into dreams of a mostly imaginary past. Dollywood's charm snuck up so effectively, it made me woozy.

I saw my boss round the corner from Showstreet, and I quickly swept my list under the counter so he wouldn't see. He greeted me and asked for a breakdown of cash, checks, and the souvenir paper money also accepted as real currency in the park. I reported the info, which he scribbled on a clipboard, and then he released me for the day.

After cleaning up, I gathered my things and locked up the *Tennessee Telephone*. I wadded up my polyester scarf, unpinned my name tag, and tossed both identifying markers into my purse. After a quick trip to drop off the cash bag, I was free to explore the park for the next few hours until Mom waddled out of Aunt Granny's on tender feet, bestrewn with okra dust like she'd been consecrated by a Southern holy man.

On my way out of Jukebox Junction, I took a right on Showstreet and passed by the sausage stand. As usual, there was a line three-deep of round-bellied middle-aged men waiting to order. I said a brief prayer for Sissy and walked past quickly, hoping a rainstorm would thunder in and drive them out of Dollywood forever.

At the fork beside the tunnel, I decided to continue toward The Village and Country Fair rather than climb the hill to Craftsman's Valley. Dolly's museum, my favorite place in the park, was just through the tunnel, but I'd been sweating all day and the last thing I wanted to hear was the slow *whoosh whoosh* of my denim-clad thighs as I made my way to the entrance. Additionally, the museum was downwind of Ham-n-Beans, a popular concession stand that churned out fart-producing pintos by the pound. I didn't want to be in its fragrant pathway this close to dinner.

Country Fair never held my interest. No matter how charming Dollywood's version of a carnival was, it would never hold a candle to Knoxville's Tennessee Valley Fair, where you could judge both prize-winning pumpkins and fist-fighting women, all named Tammy, in the same place.

The Village was better. Decorated like a turn-of-the-century town, it combined the old-timey charm of an enterprising burg with the pleasant but doomed vibe of second-class seating on the Titanic. Many people flocked to The Village's beautifully restored carousel, but the overwhelming favorite was the Dollywood Express, a real coal-fired steam locomotive that took guests on a 5-mile ride through a lush section of the property.

The train's whistle was a favorite of mine. It was irritatingly loud and minorly pitched, as lonesome sounding as a grieving mother clinging to the solid posts of the depot, awaiting her doughboy's return in a pine box. The mournful whistle was the most honest music in the park, except for Dolly's songs about childhood poverty and her *did-they-or-didn't-they* love for Porter Wagoner.

When the train pulled away from the station, the conductor would tug the horn twice, sending soot and a deep *woo wooooo* flying to the tops of the trees. My heart would clunk sadly with every toot. My sadness felt strangely familiar, like I was remembering a hardscrabble past life where I'd clung to a post of my own. Who knew what spirits were floating around the thickly wooded perimeter beyond the tracks? Most would think me silly because I believed that a psychic residue had sunk deep in this section of Dollywood long ago. What caused it was debatable, but whatever it was, it held on as strongly as the seatbelts on the Mountain Slidewinder.

After strolling past the Berries-N-Cream booth, I paused to greet the train passengers as they chugged past. I felt like the world's biggest dork waving bye-bye to a bunch of strangers. The tug in my soul told me I was only doing what came naturally, mirroring the affection I wished to receive. I didn't know if it was an Appalachian apparition beckoning me with a bittersweet memory or merely a hunger fugue created by the mouthwatering smell of Victoria's Pizza. Either way, I would spend my time here this evening.

At the east end of The Village was the Heartsong Theatre. *Heartsong* was a short immersive film about Dolly's childhood and the blazing beauty of the Smoky Mountains. When Dolly sang about flowers, for instance, fragrance would spritz from the corners of the theatre. An animatronic owl would hoot from a perch during a night scene. There was even a live banjo player dressed as Dolly's crusty mountain neighbor, Applejack, who would stagger out on stage long enough to pick out his namesake tune and then retreat. Immersive presentations were nothing new to people who frequented Anaheim and Orlando. I could count the number of theme parks I'd ever been to on one hand, though, and I found *Heartsong* truly delightful.

After a dinner of pepperoni pizza and red Powerade, I retreated into the coolness of the theatre. I sighed with contentment as the movie opened with an eagle's eye view of various scenes of the Smokies. It was easy to take East Tennessee's loveliness for granted. The quiet exclamations of the audience, many of them far from home, left me awash with fresh gratitude for my birthplace.

The only dumb part of *Heartsong* was what Sissy and I called the Butterfly Girl Scene, where a child frolicked happily in a field surrounded by animated butterflies. There was so much genuine beauty in the mountains that it seemed unnecessary to rope cartoon insects into a synchronized dance party to serve as background for the soundtrack. This wasn't the little girl's fault – she was cute as a button and doing the best with the material she had, but the scene should have been left on the cutting room floor, and the little girl recast as Dolly's tough school chum or something, the one who smarted off to the teacher and kept hand-rolled cigarettes tucked in the ruffles of her pinafore.

After the Butterfly Girl danced her way into our hearts, the movie transitioned to a section on Dolly's Christian faith. Dolly's belief in God was strong and unmistakable, never pushy. I'd seen her preach the gospel countless times just by leading with love and staying the hell out of people's business. Cynics and Bible-thumpers would say she was simply being business savvy by trying to appeal to everyone. I disagreed. If you were fortunate, you might know one or two people from whom kindness and an abiding serenity radiated constantly. I considered my daddy to be one of these people. Fred Rogers radiated the same way. Dolly was the third member of my personal Trinity.

This special kindness wasn't the same as perfection or piety. Plenty of people were good-hearted and helpful, but this trait exceeded everyday decency – it was extraordinarily rare and precious. Having known Daddy for eleven whole years before his death, I recognized that same goodness in Dolly, and I'd trounce any press agent or bulging-eyed preacher who suggested otherwise.

A sweet scene filmed in a small, white chapel followed Dolly's voiceover, and then we heard a loud crack of thunder and the sound of a torrential downpour.

Dolly, dressed in a white sequined gown, exactly like the angels on high, strode out on a porch and began to sing "He's Alive." The lyrics, though not her own, majestically proclaimed the news of Jesus' resurrection, a joyful declaration of the hope of eternal life. Her voice, backed by a mighty choir, rang true and strong.

Inside the theatre, misty rain began to fall.

Several in the audience clapped, and one person uttered a hearty, "Amen!" I didn't clap. In fact, I didn't move. I was trying my best to prevent tears from rolling out of my eyes. I felt a great ache in my soul, a longing from every flawed fiber of my being that hoped God was real and loving. There was so much evidence in my life, often unwittingly supplied by Christian authorities, that God was nothing but an imaginary pliant deity — tough when humans needed evidence of His wrath to control and oppress, but weak when it came to protecting His children, feebly giving cover to humans for failing to help the least of these.

Despite my best efforts, tears spilled down my face.

My nose started in on the fun, pouring snot so as to not be outdone by my eyes. I wiped my face on the sleeve of my button-down shirt, trying to collect myself. Crying in front of strangers was almost as embarrassing as experiencing a genuine theological moment packaged by slick corporate creatives. Normally, I was proud of my sensitivity. Infiltrating my deep longing was a quiet humiliation that Dolly's marketing team might have found the perfect sucker, one willing to transform her catharsis into a CD sale. Of course, when I really thought about it, megachurches were rarely different, willing to jerk the heartstrings of the congregation to sponsor a missionary or upgrade the sound system and coffee bar in Jesus' name.

The same psychic tug I'd felt outside suddenly occupied the nearby space, something unexplained and tremendous. The energy that settled around me was hallowed and playful –a powerful benevolence, mostly unknowable in this plane, yet sparkling with amusement for us all. And loving. So loving.

The soft rain continued for a few seconds, landing gently on my head and forearms, and then came to a stop. The energy had dissipated, too, gone as fast as it had arrived. *Heartsong* concluded with a reprise of the title track and a replay of clips from the film, and then it was over. There was more applause, and after that, we filed out into The Village.

My legs circled back of their own accord. I walked into a nearby shop and purchased the *Heartsong* album. With my employee discount, and the fact that I chose to buy an outdated cassette tape instead of a CD, the album cost next to nothing. I decided I could live with myself since I hadn't been manipulated into giving *too* much to the Dollywood coffers. As far as what had happened inside the theatre, I'd never know the answer. Maybe God – Whatever God was – popped by to remind me He was never far away, never further than the next train car or row of theme park seats, even if He always kept quiet.

Or perhaps, my pepperoni heartburn and Powerade-nourished tears, along with an effective filmmaking strategy, caused me to hallucinate so I wouldn't feel so lonely. Either way, I'd had a breakthrough.

I wasn't ready to stop believing in Something.

Dusk was approaching and the park would soon be closing. I returned to Showstreet. Sissy was busy counting her register drawer, so I sat on a bench between Sausage Works and Aunt Granny's to wait. After taking her money to the cash office, Sissy sat down next to me as we waited for Mom. Employees from other parts of the park shambled past us on their way to clock out, a zombie graveyard of glass blowers and Gibson girls and bobby soxers worn out from the day.

Eventually, Mama and the rest of Aunt Granny's spilled

out of the restaurant. Sissy and I joined the group, walking back toward Jukebox Junction and the employee entrance that would take us back to the parking lot.

"So, how was y'all's day?" Mom asked jokingly. Sissy rolled her eyes, perpetually irritated by a day filled with bratwurst bros. I snorted with laughter, grabbing Mom's reusable Daredevil Falls mug out of her hand for a sip of flat Mr. Pibb.

"Heather, did you get off early? What did you do?" Mom said to me.

I went to church was the thought I had, but I kept it inside. There was too much to explain, especially in mixed company. "Oh, nothing special," I replied. "Had some pizza and took in a show. It was a good day."

"I'm glad," she said, retrieving her mug for a long, satisfying drink.

Once outside the park, we climbed into the complementary shuttle that took us up a steep hill to the employee parking lot. Now it was time for the long drive home. Before getting into our car, I paused to look at the dimmed lights of Dollywood below, respectfully extinguished like altar candles after a sermon.

"Another day, another Dolly Dollar," I said to no one in particular.

"Get in this car, Punkinhead," Mom shouted, muffled from inside.

Tomorrow, we'd do it all again. I was eager for another religious experience. If God *was* everywhere, that would be wonderful, but if He sometimes needed a place to park it in East Tennessee, He could do worse than the contrived, sublime streets of Dollywood.

FATULOUS

I was enjoying a perfect Sunday afternoon. I sat with my legs folded under me, perched sideways on the couch in my college suite's living room. I liked to think my perch made me look cute and approachable, reminiscent of a baby swan resting beside a pond. However, I'd never seen a swan prop a bag of olestra potato chips against their wings, close by to the bathroom in case of intestinal distress caused by low-fat ingredients. Chickens, maybe, but never swans.

Open in front of me was the latest issue of *Mode* magazine. I'd first spotted the publication at the bookstore a year prior. *Mode* was a typical women's fashion rag in many respects, full of gorgeous models wearing expensive clothing sandwiched between ads for prestige skincare and jewelry, with one big exception.

All their gorgeous models were *fat*.

Each issue's cover was stamped with the same message,

"*Fashion in Sizes 12, 14, 16 ...*" The ellipsis was tantalizing, promising inclusion for every chunky honey in America. There was nothing better than wrapping myself in a cozy robe and unwrapping a guilt-free snack as I read the latest edition.

Bodies came in many shapes and sizes, even within the plus-size world. They were all beautiful. Some models were less fat than tall, magnificently solid, like strong tree trunks atop sexy legs. Others had pronounced tummies softly highlighted by pintucked trousers or A-line darting and smallish, perky bosoms, the kind that looked great in backless gowns or anything with delicate straps.

Unsurprisingly, my favorite models looked like me, viola-shaped with thick thighs and full breasts. No matter how much sand was poured in our hourglasses, we maintained the same basic curved shape, living fertility statues of sumptuousness whether clad in fatigues or formalwear.

When I saw a model with a similar body type, the usual anchor of ugliness chained to my body was temporarily yanked away, and I felt unstoppable. I had no idea our bodies could look so good! Apparently, all I needed were quality fabrics cut well and draped lusciously over my form, and I'd have a fleet of ah-ooga-eyed sailors following my every sashay, as evidenced by the photo shoots. (I really only needed one, but extra worshippers would always be welcomed.) This gave me hope I'd finally break free one day from the lingering constraints of poverty. Even *I* could buy good clothes, as long as I could pinch pennies for the next decade. Without the magazine, though, I never would have known that these fabulous clothes – and this fabulous fat-positive *lifestyle* — existed in the first place.

Thanks to *Mode,* I had gained a ton of self-esteem.

I crunched two of the weird chips in my mouth. I had another hour or so of bliss until it was time for homework. I also needed to work on getting off-book for my new theatre role. I'd been cast as Miss Furnival in *Black Comedy*. Miss Furnival was a spinster teetotaler who discovers an affection for alcohol for the first time during a neighborhood blackout. She was a fun character. After playing two male roles and both losing and finding myself in the pages of *Mode*, however, I wasn't ready to slip into old-lady territory.

There was no question I wanted to be on stage, though sometimes I wished that there weren't already several slender, attractive women in our theatre troupe. To be fair, they were older than me and the expected choices for ingenue roles. If I had to choose between non-traditional roles and not acting at all, there was no question I'd don every bad wig Cumberland owned just to be there ... but couldn't Tex, our director, throw a meaty bone to his fattest actress anyway?

I shut my magazine and sat up straight. "Yeah, *Tex*," I

said aloud to the empty suite, already channeling Norma Desmond. "Why can't you?"

I didn't want to take any opportunities away from the sweet, talented seniors, but maybe it was time to have a chat with good ole Tex. There was no reason our next play couldn't feature an all-female cast. At the very least, I could ask what I needed to do to be considered for a lead role. I wasn't the world's greatest actor or anything — I still had plenty to learn. Maybe my lack of lead roles had more to do with skill than with anything else.

Tex would be in his office right after acting class. I decided I'd pay him a visit. I liked Tex, and the feeling seemed to be mutual, but he wasn't a mentor like Ms. Houghton. That was for the best. Expecting coddling from every acting teacher would only hamstring me. The professional acting world seemed mostly indifferent and schmoozy and often cruel. I needed to practice some bravery before I was out on my own and relying on myself to pay rent, because nobody was going to advocate for me, except me.

Since that was settled, I opened *Mode* again and feasted once more. I rolled up the top of the chip bag and clipped it closed. My stomach was nervous enough now, and didn't need any nudging from the olestra.

～

AFTER CLASS, I WALKED the short distance to Tex's office. My bravado from the afternoon before had vanished in the bleary practicalities of Monday. Twice, my shaky legs changed course away from the sidewalk, insistent that I reconsider. I overrode them firmly.

I tapped twice on the wooden frame of Tex's open office door, and he waved me inside. Tex's office was messy and cozy, stuffed with books and broken props - a little bedraggled, like our theatre.

I sat down across from his desk in a scuffed yellow chair that had probably been at Cumberland since its founding. Tex folded his hands across his abdomen.

"So, what can I do for you, my dear?" His voice boomed loudly, as it usually did, a side effect of decades of stage acting.

I came right out with it. "I want to play a leading role. Will I ever do that in your theatre?"

Tex raised his eyebrows so high his forehead became a relief map of wrinkles. I gulped, wondering if I had gone too far.

"Pray tell, young lady, what exactly has brought this on?" Thankfully, I detected a hint of magnanimous amusement in his voice, and I relaxed.

"Well ... nothing, exactly. It's just that, as much as I like playing the funnies and the oldies, I want a role where I have the most lines and don't have to wear a bad wig. Miss Furnival looks like the poster child for Werther's Original."

Tex didn't reply right away. I thought I'd put my foot in it for sure. I'd learned a lot about acting, carpentry, and stage combat from him and always tried to give my best. Yet after years of effort, I wasn't one of his favorites. He was affable and decent, yet inscrutable. "I know I'm only a sophomore, and I still have a lot to learn," I quickly added, "and I very much appreciate how much I've been cast already."

Was I being courageous or crazy? I had no idea.

Tex rubbed his red beard thoughtfully. "I can't answer that," he said finally. "Do you sing?"

Despite the fact that Daddy had been a childhood violin virtuoso, sharing the stage with country legends like Archie Campbell and Minnie Pearl, I could sing about as well as a drunk divorcée yelling Helen Reddy lyrics out the sunroof of a rented limousine.

"*No,*" I answered emphatically. "Are we doing a musical next?"

"Yes," Tex answered, "*The Mikado.*"

Ugh. Gilbert and Sullivan's frenzied lyrics, no matter how lauded and whimsical, made my brain bleed. I wouldn't be auditioning for *The Mikado* even if I could sing. The realization that I would miss yet another opportunity to play the ingenue made the room recede, and I suddenly felt claustrophobic. What if I missed my chance?

"Look, kiddo," Tex began, not unkindly. "I'm not sure

what will happen in the future, but the fact of the matter is, you and I are in the same boat."

"What do you mean?"

"We're talented, we're hardworking, but we're *character actors*."

Tex smiled sympathetically before continuing. "Why do you think I love directing? Because I get to call the shots. No casting director is going to look at me and think, 'leading man.' And likely, they're going to think the same about you because of your body shape."

I sat, stunned. A thousand different emotions churned inside my chest – shame, confusion, sadness. I wasn't sure if it was fair to be angry. Tex wasn't trying to be vicious; he was only sharing his experience. His dreams of success, probably similar to mine, had been trampled at some point. He was actually offering a roadmap, such as it was.

As we sat in silence, I realized I *was* angry. I was *furious* with the lack of imagination in the world, irascibly aware of the superficial bureaucracy present in every facet of our society. Who the hell had the right to tell me, or Tex, that we didn't fit into some unattainable standard?

In fact, Tex was handsome. His face was trustworthy and gently noble. He looked believable seated upon a throne or at the helm of a ship. What more did these purveyors of perfection want?

"Those people are stupid, then," I said, voice trembling. "There are way more normal people than there are perfect people. We fall in love and have adventures too, you know."

"I agree," Tex replied, "but I decided a long time ago not to let it bother me. It's not good, it's not bad. It simply is what it is."

"For now," I said defiantly. He might've been completely right, but I refused to take his word for it. I softened my tone, not wanting to be disrespectful. "I hope it will change."

"I hope it does, too," he answered. He didn't seem especially ready to tear down any barriers.

I'd traveled as far as I could with Tex for now. "I've bugged you enough for one day," I told him as I stood to leave. "Thank you for listening."

"You're welcome," Tex said sincerely. "Anytime."

I moped back to Asher Hall. Carlene and Ana were home, watching TV in the living area.

"Is everything ok?" Ana asked. "You look sad."

"I'm fine," I said, opening the door to my and Dylan's room and tossing my backpack on the floor. "It's just some bullshit."

I couldn't see their faces as I stepped out of my stiff sneakers, but I knew they were looking at each other with interest.

"Girl," said Carlene, "get out here. You can't just say that and then retreat into your dorm dungeon."

I left my room and sat down at the small dining table beside them. "I talked to my theatre director today and asked him if he thought he'd ever cast me in a lead role. He told me he wasn't sure, which was fair. Then, he said that since both of us were *character actors*," I emphasized sarcastically, "we'd likely never be cast as leads, especially me, especially because of my body size."

Carlene and Ana gasped. "You can't be serious!" Carlene cried. "That's the dumbest thing I ever heard!"

"I know he has years of experience with auditions and audiences or whatever, but is it really earth-shattering to cast the fat girl as the strong badass? Or the object of affection?"

"Of course not," they said.

"And let's get something straight," I added. "I may be fat, but I'm also cute. I come from a good-looking family. So, I'm not sure I'm in the same category as a character actor who plays a weathered mobster with no teeth. Fat doesn't equal ugly."

"Testify, girl!" Carlene drawled. Carlene, also plus-sized, had a cute retroussé nose and crystal blue bedroom eyes that could put the content of a man's trousers in traction, if she looked at him just right. I was grateful for her support.

"You shouldn't listen to him or anyone else who tries to dim your shine," Ana said. "Keep going until you get what you want."

That was solid advice. "Thank you, my friend."

"And by the way, gordita, you and Carlene are beautiful. Don't you forget it."

"What's that mean? Gordita?"

"It's an affectionate nickname for chubby girls. We're not obsessed with skinny back home. Lots of women are bigger and we celebrate it in the D.R. The men celebrate it, too."

"Remind me to renew my passport!" exclaimed Carlene.

"So, you and Carlene are my gorditas."

I loved nicknames, and this one lit up my soul. I'd never heard the equivalent in my saltine-white culture because no such word existed. When it came to cracker fat, there was only self-loathing, the loathing of other fatties, and perpetual dieting.

"That is one of the nicest things anyone has ever said to me," I told Ana. "Thank you."

"You're welcome. Now, stop wasting time on what one person thinks and watch this movie with us."

I sat down on the floor in front of the couch, taking her advice on both counts.

~

NOT LONG AFTER MY meeting with Tex, I sat in a cozy corner of the library reading entertainment magazines. Awards season was imminent, and I hadn't missed a televised event in years. I enjoyed the fashion and speeches, imagining myself someday teetering carefully down the red carpet on designer heels, gushingly promoting my movie about a visually impaired war orphan who wins a beauty pageant, then raiding the nominees' gift room and taking extra while everyone else sat watching Billy Crystal sing parodies of the year's best picture nods in the main auditorium of the Dorothy Chandler Pavilion.

The Primetime Emmy® awards would be held soon, and I'd be watching. My favorite guilty pleasure, *The Young and the Restless*, swept the Daytime show earlier in the year, so I'd already had my fill of winning. Soap operas were ridiculous, but Mama and I had been watching *The Young and the Restless* since 1984, when Nikki was a stripper and Victor was forced into a piranha tank by some bad guys. It was a rare art form. Soap actors not only memorized pages of dialogue every day, but they also managed to infuse believable emotionality into story lines so preposterous that even the most loyal viewer would sometimes huff, "Oh, for Pete's sake," at the sight of yet another hunk with amnesia.

I wasn't rooting for any particular primetime actor, or so I thought. As I perused the list of nominees in my magazine, one picture stood out from the rest. Camryn Manheim, a first-time nominee for Best Supporting Actress in a Drama Series for her role on the law drama *The Practice*, had long chestnut hair and a fuller face than all the actresses on NBC's Must-See TV combined. I brought the magazine in for a closer look.

Is she fat? I wondered. I couldn't tell by the headshot alone. *A young, plus-size nominee. That would be amazing.*

She was pretty, too, reminding me of a hip auntie who would let you borrow her leather jacket and not narc to your mom if you showed up at her door drunk at 3:00 am. I scribbled the name of the show in my notebook and promised myself I'd watch it. I needed all the encouragement I could get. I'd felt uncomfortable around Tex since our meeting, and I was focused on re-establishing the status quo with him. I lived, ate, and breathed Miss Furnival and tried to keep my opinions to myself.

A few evenings later, I escaped rehearsal early enough to catch an episode of *The Practice.* It turned out, Camryn Manheim *was* fat, and her character, attorney Ellenor Frutt, looked cool and acted cool. Who on Earth was this chick? And why had I never heard of her?

I finished the episode nearly in tears, happy to see such a vibrant and beautiful representation of a woman like me on TV. I wanted to know more about Camryn. What was her story? How did she become a success? I instinctively knew she'd had similar struggles. Who or what gave her the strength to keep trying?

One thing was for sure – now I had someone to root for.

The night of the awards show, I power-walked so quickly, so breathlessly back to the dorm from rehearsal, friction almost wore a hole in the inner thighs of my jeans. Luckily, I didn't miss much.

When I was finally able to sit down and watch, I paid close attention to the audience, scanning the room for Camryn Manheim to see what she was wearing. At first, she wasn't visible. Sheath dresses were a popular choice for the women, silk and satin toothpaste tubes vacuum-sealed to actresses with non-existent body fat. I wondered how many weeks of carb-less torture they'd endured to look picture-perfect on the red carpet, and how many of them would avail themselves of the nearest cheese-stuffed item as soon as the broadcast was over. These goddesses had my deepest sympathy as well as my disdain at not keeping a few loose cashews or something stashed in their Judith Leiber evening bags.

I saw Camryn. She was dressed in a low-cut black dress with double spaghetti straps and an elaborate diamond necklace that looked like it had been lifted off the snoring form of an elderly European princess. A sheer black wrap hugged her shoulders, probably to cover a part of her arms she felt self-conscious about, and her updo was well-executed, likely full of enough hairpins to set off a dozen metal detectors. All in all, she looked gorgeous.

When it was time for her category, I sat with bated breath

as the nominees were listed. Although I wasn't sure if it would do any good, I sent up a prayer, too. Then, her name was announced as the winner! Well, sort of. Mark Harmon called her Carmen instead of Camryn, but at least he got her last name right.

I clapped loudly and whistled at the TV. Camryn Manheim climbed the stairs to the podium, surprised as anyone and grinning from ear-to-ear. I turned up the volume so I wouldn't miss a word of her speech. She thanked her parents, her fellow nominees, and various show-biz people who'd helped along the way. Then, she held up a red autograph book she'd brought, asking her peers to sign. I laughed, overjoyed for her.

The camera captured shots of the other nominees reacting to her win, and her speech seemed to be over ... but just when I thought she was finished, she erupted again in delight.

"This is for all the fat girls!" she yelled mightily, thrusting her award towards the sky.

My mouth dropped open in shock. Happy tears tumbled out of my eyes as if they'd been waiting to jump. I clapped some more, moving my hands so rapidly my palms turned red. She was sharing her success with *us,* with every single fat girl, and the one standing in her dorm room, systematically made to feel small but forever dreaming of big things, resoundingly *accepted.*

I spread the word to my suitemates, unable to refrain from interrupting their studies, punching the air with triumph as if I'd KO'd a Russian boxer.

By the end of the show, I'd settled down enough to get ready for bed. I tried to fall asleep. I was still ecstatic. The moment Camryn Manheim lifted her award into the air, looking every inch like Lady Liberty, I felt renewed hope that anything was possible. I had a new role model now, a misfit lodestar who was lighting the way for the rest of us.

I decided there was no longer any room for naysayers. True, I wasn't much of a runner, but I still had what it took to compete. I'd win this marathon, one step at a time.

THE NEXT MORNING, I awoke refreshed and ready to take on the world. The early-autumn leaves of Kentucky, tinted golden by the sun, reminded me of the trophies I might one day win. I felt self-assured and comfortable as I flitted across campus, a perky bumblebee with the intention of sampling every flower.

After two morning classes, I headed to the computer lab tucked away on the second floor of the Bennett Building. I wanted to read reaction about Camryn Manheim's big night to see if other people were as thrilled as I was. I didn't have a computer of my own. The lab was wired for DSL, the fastest internet speed available, leaving the dial-up I was used to in Knoxville in the dust. I typed my student ID number into the sign-in screen and waited for the desktop to load.

Finally, I was able to surf the web. I clicked on Internet Explorer and went to the browser home page. I typed her name into the search bar. Four pages of results popped up, including one for her website. I clicked on it immediately.

Camryn Manheim's website was thorough, but not so full of pictures that it would take a long time to load. I read through her biography and filmography, adding a couple of the movies – *movies!* — in which she'd appeared to my list. I found out she'd gotten her start onstage, loved theatre, and even produced a one-woman show about the bias and difficulty she'd experienced because of her body size – a body size, one might add, that was hardly uncommon in the world.

A tantalizing "Contact Us" button caught my eye. I clicked on it. An empty email chat box appeared. The intended purpose of the contact page was clearly meant for professional inquiries, but I couldn't help myself. I typed a gushing fan letter to Camryn, describing our similarities and sending congratulations for her groundbreaking win. I doubt she'd ever see it, as it was unlikely anyone even remotely famous would monitor their own fan mail, but the act of writing itself was a prayer of thanks.

I pressed SEND and went on my way.

Back at Asher Hall, I gathered all my issues of *Mode* to reread. During freshman year at Cumberland, I'd lined my dorm walls with dozens of pictures of my favorite actors and musicians. The constant upkeep of re-taping pictures to a porous concrete wall, as well as the feeling of exposure while undressing in front of a room full of staring celebrities, made me reconsider when I'd moved back in. I'd taped nothing to the walls this year.

I thought it might be a good time to reassess. Maybe I should choose a glamorous woman or two for inspiration. Surely, *People* would publish a list of winners, and I could snag a picture of Camryn holding her golden statuette.

I flipped through the issues. Nothing stood out. Every pictorial and most of the ads were beautifully photographed, but it was impractical and boring to tear out all of them and cover the whole wall, repeating what I'd done the previous year. I wasn't sure how to proceed. It was almost time for rehearsal, anyway. I left the project for another day, hugely content overall.

～

THE WEEKS TICKED BY, and things were going well. Miss Furnival was a boozy hit. I'd made peace with the character weeks before, just glad to be onstage. The audience's reaction energized me, every uproarious laugh an egocentric mainline injected right into my veins. God, it felt good. Live performance, even in a ratty theatre with turd-colored walls, was a thrilling absurdity, an electrifying contract between performers and observers, meant to entertain as well as edify. There was nothing edifying about Miss Furnival except her hairdo — which served as a cautionary tale when choosing a stylist – yet I was still creating art.

Next semester, I'd be offstage because of the musical. I'd soaked up as much energy as possible to get me through the dry spell. I figured I would work on my wardrobe and self-esteem in the meantime. I hadn't given up on convincing Tex that I deserved to be a leading lady. Hopefully, he would consider the possibility between now and the next time I was cast — if there was a next time.

I couldn't believe it was already December. Finals would start soon, and afterwards, I'd be back in Knoxville for three blissful weeks of break. Toward the end of each semester, campus would become a much quieter place as students began to study. Part of our preparation involved a mental pulling up of stakes, like a group of ringmasters and acrobats who'd come to town but were eager not to overstay their welcome. The psychological unhitching of graduating seniors from the underclassmen was especially apparent, the seniors capable only of distracted interactions as if they were already gone from this world, muddy wheel ruts carved deep in the fairgrounds as farewell.

I'd come to enjoy this bittersweet feeling. There was a big difference between taking on expected responsibility after college and being crushed with it during childhood. Each change of semester brought new beginnings and endings, and the ritual soothed me. I was grateful for the buffer Cumberland provided, and I had real hope I'd have a defined path forward by Graduation Day.

There was just enough time to check my email and surf the web for a few minutes before walking back to the dorm to start writing my final paper for Linguistics. I had two new emails, probably from the college about upcoming deadlines. I clicked on the first one, which listed special dining hall hours for finals week.

The second email had a subject line I didn't recognize. I clicked into it, thinking it might be from Mom. Mom enjoyed learning about new technology, if it was fun. Thanks to Sissy, she had learned to use email — mostly. A wacky subject line here, a totally blank message there. Despite learning how to type in high school, Mom found keyboarding more difficult for some reason, treating capitalization as a suggestion and removing spaces between words as if a telegram office was charging her by the inch. I braced myself.

Thank you for your lovely letter and kind words, I read. *It means a lot to me.*

I'll keep the torch up high!

Happy Holidays.

Cheers,

Camryn

"Oh my *God!*" I said aloud, earning a scornful stare from a girl next to me.

I wasn't sure if her scorn was due to the noise or the blasphemy. "Sorry," I whispered.

Camryn Manheim — or someone on her staff — had written me back! I did a little dance in my seat, tapping my feet as quietly as I could. The reigning Best Supporting Actress in a Drama Series, star of stage and screen, and plus-size *royalty* had granted a reply. I was euphoric. My newly discovered pride from earlier in the year came roaring back, faster than Miss Furnival sucking back a Jell-O shot in the brief cover of darkness between lightning strikes and louder than the cheers of a standing ovation.

This was a sign, a technological manifestation of my desire to be known. I'd never give up now. I pressed PRINT and watched a piece of paper slide smoothly out of the machine in the corner. I retrieved it and placed it carefully in a notebook pocket. I couldn't wait to show my friends.

I walked back to Asher, making it back to our suite in

under ten minutes. The time to write the Linguistics paper was upon me, but I had one more task to complete before starting.

Inspiration had struck. I retrieved an issue of *Mode* from my desk. Flipping back to an ad I'd seen before, I carefully tore it from the magazine and fished around my desk for a roll of masking tape, the only adhesive allowed on the dorm walls. Masking tape was a terrible adherent, and ironically, pretty much useless for masking, but it was perfect for my current project.

I tore off a piece of tape and rubbed it firmly across part of the text on the page. Then, I took a pen and scribbled something new on top. Pleased with my new artwork, I tore off another big piece of tape and looped it on the back for hanging.

On display in the ad were several beautiful curvaceous bodies wearing a famous plus-size brand's new bra and underwear line. The ad proclaimed them "fabulous," and I agreed, to a point.

I thought it was time we had a more apt descriptor. We were beautiful; we were strong; we were unapologetically glorious — comfortable in our own skins and unbothered with the need for approval even as we awaited inescapable adoration from lovers and friends.

We were undeniable.

I slapped the paper on the back of the suite door as a reminder to myself and others, ready for whatever was next.

"*Fatulous!*" the ad now read, and I truly was.

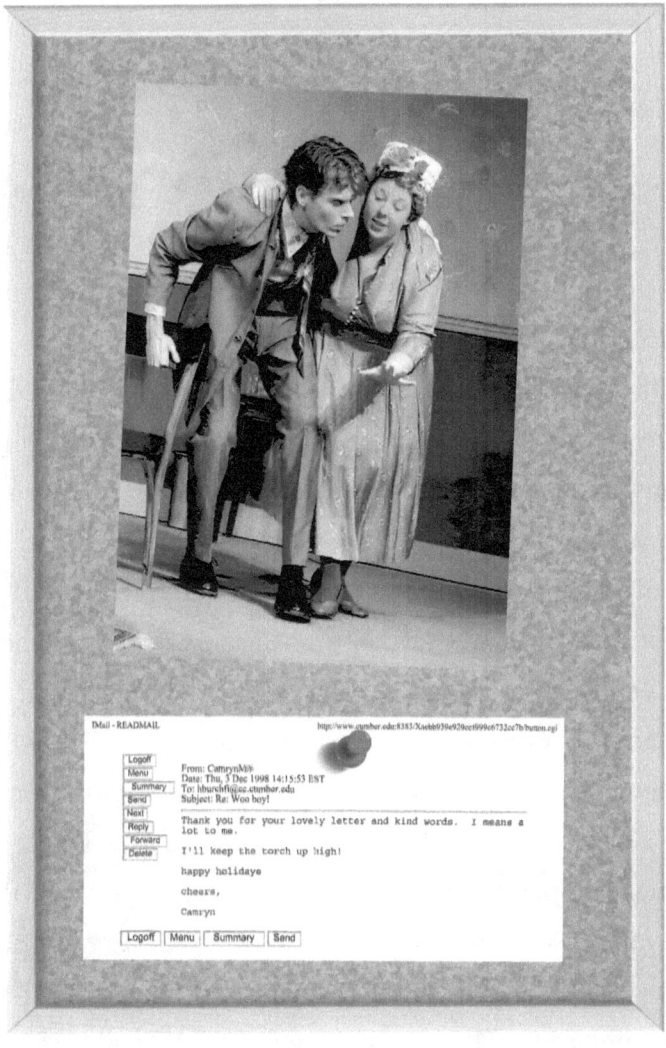

I was sick. By the start of holiday break, I'd become a tight-chested, congested mess. I'd always had to be careful with colds. Asthma often turned a boring case of the sniffles into a week-long albuterol marathon, followed by a week of hawking up phlegm that sounded exactly like a long-haired cat yakking up furballs.

Having a chest cold was miserable, but at least I had fallen ill at the start of break rather than during Christmas, which was still a few days away. Last semester had been a slog. I'd finally been cast again after stage managing *The Mikado*, although in a bit role. We'd just wrapped up a production of *The Haunting of Hill House*, where I'd played Mrs. Dudley, a dumbass housekeeper who was terrified enough to inform anyone in shouting distance that she wouldn't work past dusk because of the demonic horrors inside, but not terrified enough to quit. Mrs. Dudley annoyed me. If I had to choose between working in a haunted house and starvation, I'd choose starvation, hands down. Only stupid people stuck around a place where ghosts could eat their faces or spookily bind them to a mop, for all eternity, to sop up the endless ectoplasm.

Even worse, Dylan had graduated early, leaving me without a roommate for next semester. I was proud of her accomplishments, but I was going to miss her a lot. Though only a junior, I felt as though my own graduation was imminent, probably due to the flurry of excited energy in our room during the last few weeks. I wasn't ready for things to change.

Dylan's goldfish felt the same way. Packing to leave school wasn't the same as tossing an overnight bag into the car or taking home extra laundry to wash after finals. Dylan had been at Cumberland for four years, and everything from her stereo to the funky leftover perfume sample from the freshman orientation bag had to be jammed into a box or garbage can.

Dylan packed for several days. One evening, after studying, I flipped to a rerun while Dylan transferred clothes from the closet into a large duffel bag. Most of her side of the room had already been cleared, leaving only Aslan, Dylan's goldfish, as sole decoration on top of the chest of drawers.

I'd miss Aslan, too. His was a peaceful life, swimming around his big bowl in no particular hurry, a song of *bloop*

bloop forever on his lips. When Dylan went home for the weekend, I'd carefully sprinkle a capful of food into his bowl as directed, watching him rise to the top to gobble it. Sometimes, I'd ask him if his food was good, even though I was pretty sure fish didn't have ears.

Being responsible for any other living creature besides myself made me feel uneasy and incapable. I wasn't sure if I'd ever want kids. I was already high strung; I knew I'd be an unbearably neurotic mother, the kind who'd have to breathe into the brown paper bag before I packed Junior's lunch in it.

I was focused on the TV and at first didn't hear what Dylan had said.

"Where's Aslan?" she asked again. She was holding the plastic bottle of fish food, ready to feed him supper.

"What do you mean, where's Aslan? Is he not in his bowl?"

Dylan stepped to the side of the chest of drawers, revealing a bowl full of water – but no fish.

Our expressions of shock mirrored each other, and I leapt up from the bed.

"Oh, my Lord! Where did he go? We've got to find him before he drowns!" I exclaimed.

Dylan flung open the top drawer, quickly but carefully shaking out socks and underwear trying to find him. "Did he jump out of the bowl?" she said in bewilderment. "Where are you, Aslan?"

The top drawer yielded nothing but Victoria's secrets and an old comb. Dylan repeated her actions in the drawer below, working faster, but again came up empty-handed.

"Where he is?" she said, crestfallen. "Fish don't just disappear into thin air. Where's my little buddy?" she asked frantically, now wildly rummaging around the lowest drawer.

I got on all fours and slowly pushed the chest forward, checking to see if he'd fallen backwards, not wanting to flatten him in case he was nearby.

"Here, fishie fishie fishie," I said urgently.

"He can't hear you!" Dylan wailed.

Aslan wasn't behind the chest of drawers, either. I helped Dylan look around the foot of her bed. Soon, we'd exhausted all possibilities.

"I am genuinely baffled," Dylan said. "That is the weirdest thing that's ever happened in this dorm room. Poor little guy."

"I'm really sorry," I replied. "I hope he didn't suffer, wherever he is."

Dylan took Aslan's bowl from the top of the chest and walked into the bathroom. I followed her. She poured its contents into the tub. The water swirled down the drain, trailed by a tiny fake cave that fell out with a plop.

"I was worried about having to transport him home in a Ziploc bag," she said. "I guess that problem's solved."

"Are you going to keep his bowl?" I asked.

"Do you want it?"

"Um, no. I was just checking. Thank you, though."

"I guess I should get rid of it," Dylan sniffed. "I feel weird just chucking it into the dumpster. What if he comes back?"

We both started to giggle, but respectfully, as befitting a symbolic burial at sea.

"I am truly sorry for your loss and this odd turn of events. If nothing else, this will make a great story to tell everyone at your graduation party."

"You don't think it ... means anything, do you?"

"Maybe it means Aslan was trying to keep you from leaving," I said, turning my lower lip under to give her an exaggerated sad face. "Instead of hiding, he accidentally catapulted himself into an alternate dimension. We should probably call the Physics Department."

Dylan laughed again, a delightful sound that ran up the scale like someone tinkling piano keys. I was going to miss her laugh, too. She'd become a good friend.

"No, I don't think it means anything, except that you're going to kick ass in the real world," I told her truthfully.

"Thank you," Dylan said sweetly. She fanned her misty eyes. "Ok, ok. Enough mushy stuff. I've got to finish packing."

"And I've got to finish this rerun."

"What are you going to do with all this extra space next semester?" asked Dylan. "You'll have room for anything."

"Fish séance," I replied. "I'll let you know how it goes."

~

I STILL WASN'T ANY better after two days in bed. My lungs were crackly and irritated, and the expectorant I chugged every four hours hadn't done much to break up the congestion. I'd camped out on the couch, propped up on pillows to sleep because lying down made it harder to breathe.

I couldn't sleep, though. There was a nagging fear in the back of my mind. I couldn't remember ever being so sick or so constantly out of breath. Going to the doctor was the obvious solution, but I had a hard stop programmed into my brain that prevented me from seeking out healthcare unless absolutely necessary.

I was worse than an old dog that needed every pill wrapped in lunch meat. I'd dreaded doctors' visits since childhood. Every time we'd gotten off the bus at Dameron Avenue, where the Knox County Health Department was located, I'd cry full-throated with dread. I'd never had a health department nurse or pediatrician treat me with anything resembling affection or long-term interest in my well-being. That was another side effect of being poor. The nurses at the health department were downright mean, too busy to address my abject terror of needles or offer even a moment's comfort or explanation before throwing a dart into my deltoid.

Parents and children suffered in silence at any county health department, afraid to rock the boat, forcing themselves to appear appropriately humbled as to earn their free care. The best a poor kid could hope for at the health department was a no-name bandage and a brittle, generic sticker that fell off immediately and got crushed under the heels of the other poverty-stricken folks in the waiting room.

Mom decided to splurge on a private doctor after one too many patronizing encounters. Our whole family became patients of Dr. Lithgow right before I started middle school. Dr. Lithgow was an easy-going physician with a mountain hiker vibe. His practice was conveniently located across the street from Kmart, a must for the average no-frills South Knoxvillian. I liked Dr. Lithgow a hundred times better than any other doctor I'd had, but we still treated him like an extravagance, because we couldn't afford health insurance and visits to his office were rarely in our budget. Thankfully, he'd never made me feel self-conscious about my size, although I feared he was merely saving his weight loss lecture for when I was older.

Between health department trauma, lack of money, and the deferred-but-soon-due fat lecture, I would practically have to be dying before I returned to the doctor.

I spent the afternoon of December 22nd drifting in and out of a fitful and restless nap on the couch. I was exhausted and weak, unable to sleep deeply enough to recover. A terrible sci-fi movie droned in the background, but I wasn't paying attention. I wasn't hungry. I wasn't thirsty. I was miserable.

Mom brought me a hot mug of tea. "Heather, honey, you need to go to the doctor. I know you don't want to, but you have to. How's your breathing?"

"Not so good," I admitted weakly. "Would you make me an appointment?"

Mom picked up the phone and dialed Dr. Lithgow's office. "I'm going to talk to his nurse. Maybe she can give us some advice in the meantime." I slowly lowered my legs to the floor and walked to the bathroom. When I returned, Mom was already talking to someone.

"Yes, she has asthma. Yes, she uses an inhaler." Mom turned toward me. "Heather, she wants to know how many times you've used your inhaler today." I tried to remember. Was she asking from this morning or including last night when I couldn't sleep? My thinking was soupy.

"I don't know. A lot."

Mom relayed the message. "What?" she asked the nurse. "The hospital?"

I heard the word *hospital* and my throat shrunk to the size of a drinking straw. Oh my God, was it that serious? I inhaled with a wheeze, then exhaled. My exhale was shallower than before, like a python had wrapped itself around my torso. I was terrified at my sudden decompensation.

"Mom, I can't breathe," I said urgently. "I can't breathe."

"I have to go," Mom said. "I need to call an ambulance."

Ambulance tore through my mind like a bullet. Was I going to die?

Instinctively, I pitched forward, touching my chest to my knees. The movement helped me gulp a lungful of air, and I relaxed the tiniest bit. I stayed like that as Mom called 911. I was frozen with fear. People died from asthma attacks all the time. This was by far the worst I'd ever had.

Mom sat next to me on the couch, her hand resting on my upper back.

"How are you doing, honey?" she asked. "Are you any worse?"

I was very frightened. I wanted to cry, but I knew it would only make breathing harder. My stomach quivered, too, and I felt like I might lose control of my bowels if something didn't improve. I focused my gaze on individual tufts of our thin, stained carpet, trying to sidestep the panic long enough to take another breath.

I shook my head. "I don't think so."

Sissy quickly gathered our purses and coats as Mom and I waited on the couch. Within minutes, the ambulance arrived. One male and one female paramedic entered the trailer, both carrying nylon medic bags. They asked some questions and then stuck a small device over my index finger.

"This measures how much oxygen you've got in your blood," the female paramedic said. "Let's see how you're doing."

After a few seconds, the monitor beeped. The screen read 89.

"Go get the stretcher," she told the other paramedic.

"Am I going to the hospital?"

"Yes ma'am," she said briskly. "Her pulse ox is low," she said to Mom. "A normal reading is 95 or above."

"That can't be right," Mom frowned.

My heart lurched in my chest, beating double time. The feeling of suffocation was back. My exhaustion kept the panic slightly subdued as they wrestled each other, like a gas pedal and brake pressed at the same time.

Before I knew it, the male paramedic had threaded a tube into my nose. "We're going to give you some oxygen, ok? This will help you breathe a little better," he said. The oxygen felt cool and smelled like the disposable plastic it was made from. The paramedics helped me onto the stretcher, then wheeled me down the trailer stairs and into the back of the ambulance. They placed a blanket over me, but as soon as the cold air hit my feet, I realized I wasn't wearing shoes.

"Sissy and I are right behind you, Heather Pooh," Mom

called over the noise of the idling engine. The oxygen was helping. As my breathing began to ease, my mind grasped for anything positive. I'd noticed the paramedics had turned off the red flashing lights, and I took that as a sign of encouragement, until I remembered that the ambulance that pulled up to our apartment the night Daddy died had them turned off, too.

The closest hospital was Parkwest, but we decided on UT Medical Center since Dr. Lithgow had privileges there. UT was the largest hospital in Knoxville and not necessarily the best. On the plus side, it had no religious affiliation like Baptist or St. Mary's. I loved God plenty, but I didn't trust any place that infused what should have been solely science-driven treatment with phrases like, "God spoke to me about you," or "I believe the Holy Spirit will guide me." I wasn't so sure about that. The only thing I wanted helping to guide my doctor was a nurse who graduated summa cum laude and the latest million-dollar robotic surgical machine.

God knew I was weak, frantic, and frightened. What I needed from Him right now was to heal me as quickly as possible without any professional proselytization.

We arrived at UT fifteen minutes later. The paramedics wheeled me into a large room with several bays cordoned off by curtains. "We're going to leave the oxygen on you for now," the female paramedic said. "Are you still doing ok?"

"I'm doing ok," I answered. "Thank you for helping me."
"You're welcome," she said, patting my foot with her gloved hand. "The doctor will be right in. Feel better."

My rescuer drew the blue curtain closed on two sides, leaving me without much of a view, and then exited through the automatic doors where we'd entered. I studied the curtain, wondering who was responsible for choosing the color. The hue was perfectly medium, not crisp enough for French blue nor cheerful enough for sky blue nor dark enough to be patriotic. There was no pattern overlaying it, no soothing stripe of ocean aqua, no helpful navy meant to hide stains — only a boring and charmless middle-of-the-road blue that evoked chain hotel décor and baggy prison jumpsuits.

This impersonal detail frightened me. Was it the same blue of the sheets they used to cover the faces of people who'd died? I hoped the doctor would hurry.

Within seconds, the doctor scraped back the curtain and walked up to my bed. He looked pleasant and competent. After asking a few questions, he listened to my chest with a stethoscope and checked my pulse ox again.

"I think this virus has put you pretty far down a hole as far as your asthma's concerned. We're going to take some imaging to check for pneumonia, but we're going to work on your breathing first. Have you ever had a breathing treatment?" he asked.

"No, what's that?"

"We'll give you some nebulized albuterol to inhale over a few minutes. It will reach farther and work faster than your inhaler. That should help. I'll send in the nurse to set it up."

"Thank you, doctor."

He didn't sound especially worried. I thought that was a good sign, unless he underplayed the seriousness on purpose, wanting to talk to Mom first.

I shook my head trying to dislodge the thought, managing to knock loose one of the oxygen prongs in my nostril. That was stupid, I decided. I was a bona fide adult — on paper, anyway – and practitioners weren't allowed to blab someone's medical information without permission. Plus, Mom wasn't the best person to break that kind of news to, unless the doctor didn't care if she gathered her purse to leave and called them a "know-nothin' butthead" in the middle of it.

The nurse came in holding a plastic doodad that looked like a futuristic flute. Attached to it was a tiny cup filled with liquid and several feet of plastic tubing.

"Hi, honey," the nurse said. "I've got your breathing treatment." She disconnected my oxygen, unthreading the prongs from my nose, and plugged the new tubing into one of the special outlets behind my head. Immediately, the flute part began to steam like dry ice in a heavy metal video. "You're going to put this into your mouth and breathe normally until it's empty. This should get those lungs nice and open."

"Ok. Thank you." I took the flute from her and put it in my mouth. I inhaled as deeply as I could. The steam tasted medicinal but not bad. On my fourth inhale, I felt a popping sensation in my lower chest area, and part of the invisible weighted band crushing my torso eased for the first time in days.

"I can already tell a difference," I croaked with relief.

"That's great," she smiled. "Now put that back in your mouth."

I followed her instructions for a few seconds. "Is my mom here yet? Can you send her in?" I asked quickly.

"I'll go check. You might start to feel a little shaky. If you do, don't be worried. The breathing treatment can cause that."

I was just beginning to experience what she'd described, although it wasn't yet unpleasant. Since I'd barely slept for days, the albuterol only made me alert, and I felt as though I could write a paper with the energy I'd suddenly gained. I inhaled again, deeper this time, and more of the squeezing fell away.

I fell back against the raised head of the bed. *Thank you, God, thank you everybody* I prayed in gratitude.

Mom popped her head in between the curtains. "Hey, Heather Pooh. Can I come in?"

I nodded yes since the breathing flute was in place. There were no chairs and no TV in my area, only the bed. She stood close and tried to smooth down my hair.

"I talked to the nurse for a minute. Are you feeling better?" Mom asked.

I nodded yes again. "This is helping," I said with half my mouth. "They're going to take an x-ray next to make sure I don't have pneumonia."

"Pneumonia? Good *Lord*," Mom grimaced. I knew she was thinking of the cost if I had to be admitted or needed expensive drugs. Mom's reaction was automatic, and even though she didn't mean to add to my burden, I felt a hot beam of stress zap my tired mind. A pile of medical bills could ruin any of us for years to come, which was part of the reason we hardly ever went to the doctor — it cost too damn much to get sick, or to get better. We'd mostly relied on home remedies and our piebald Appalachian genetics to fill in the gaps up to this point, but our luck had run out. Now that the fear of immediate death had retreated, my focus shifted to affordability, my default setting.

I shrugged, both in acknowledgement and as an answer. What was the alternative? Die for lack of treatment? Thank God there were laws guaranteeing the right to emergency care without upfront payment.

Mom would work herself into an early grave to give me

the care I needed. I just hated to see it on her face. She'd resigned herself to a lifetime of back-breaking labor long before I was born, and even if Sissy or I became wealthy one day and tried to take care of her, I was afraid the look of despair would always remain, still plainly visible beneath a pair of designer shades and an expensive sun hat.

I would've given anything to erase her trauma. It was likely the only thing I'd inherit, besides the family picture albums.

"Do you need anything right now?" I shook my head no. "Will you be ok if I go back and sit with Sissy?" I nodded. There was no point in her staying – I couldn't talk and there was no place for her to sit. I gave her a thumbs up and she left.

The flute stopped smoking a few minutes later. I checked the little cup, which was now empty, and set the whole contraption aside. My breathing wasn't perfect, but it was good enough to quiet the terror. I could handle being bored. The nurse came back a while later, asked me how I was, and again told me I'd soon be going for an x-ray.

I tried to snooze. The albuterol made it hard. The medicine buzzed through me, running laps in my bloodstream. I didn't care, even though I needed to sleep. At least I could breathe.

More time passed. An orderly came in and wheeled me through a bunch of hallways for the x-ray. The Emergency Department seemed miles away. In the cold and cheerless imaging suite, I posed several times – with lifted arms, from the side, holding my breath — while the technician took the pictures. It was over quickly, and I was returned to my curtain cubicle.

The nurse entered again with two bags of IV fluid. She explained one was for hydration. The other contained a steroid to help decrease the inflammation in my lungs and help the albuterol work better. I'd never had an IV, and it was a most inconvenient time for a christening. Too bad.

"I've never had an IV before and I hate needles," I told the nurse. "I know I need to be brave, though." I stuck out my arm and squinched my eyes shut. "Just warn me before you stick it in."

"I will," she said. I opened my eyes for a peek. The nurse had an aura of capability, of unshakable efficiency, preparing the kit and swiping my arm with alcohol in one graceful movement. I admired her proficiency even in my fatigued and fearful state.

"On 'three,' you'll feel a pinch, ok?"

My eyes slammed shut and I leaned back against the bed. I felt the sharp sting of the needle for a second, then it disappeared. "Don't look yet," she said. There was rustling and the sensation of something tugging my arm as she patted a wide strip of tape across the crook. "All done," she announced.

I leaned over to inspect my arm. "Can I move it?" I asked.

"Sure, just be careful."

I rotated my wrist and made a fist. "That wasn't so bad. Thank you."

"You're welcome. We're still waiting for your x-ray results. The doctor will be back then."

"Can you please ask my mom to come here?"

"Will do."

Now that I was alone, the cool trickling sensation from the IV was very noticeable. When I focused on it, I felt a little woozy. Riding shotgun with the woozy feeling was my old nemesis anxiety, ready to hijack the driver's seat and shuttle me right back to panic. Luckily, Mom returned.

"How's it going, Punkinhead?"

I held out my arm to her. "Look. My first IV. I did good."

"What's in it?"

"Hydration and a steroid to reduce the inflammation in my lungs. I'm starting to feel better. I really am."

"Praise God," Mom muttered. "Do they know about the x-ray yet?"

"X-rays. They took a bunch. No, but hopefully the results will be back when this is finished. The nurse did a good job. I can't even feel the IV unless I think about it."

"Well, don't do that," said Mom in the tone of voice she used to scold my boy cousins for belching on command. She knew how susceptible I was to negative suggestion. "You've had an IV before, by the way — that time you were jumping on the couch chewing on a toothbrush and fell on your face. They had to stitch up the inside of your mouth. Thank the Lord you didn't poke your eyeball out."

I'd been three at the time. "Exactly where were you when this circus audition went wrong?" I sassed.

"In the kitchen," Mom answered. "I should have taken the toothbrush with me. On the other hand, you never tried to do it again."

The curtain opened once more, and the doctor strolled in.

"Good news," he said. "No pneumonia." Mom and I exhaled in relief. "How are you feeling?"

"Better. Exhausted." I told him.

"I'm going to send you home with some prescriptions. You'll need to take steroids for a week to keep that lung inflammation down, and a stronger expectorant ... an antibiotic to be on the safe side ... and I want you to start using a preventative inhaler along with your albuterol."

In my head, I heard the yodeling music from *The Price is Right*. On the show, if the contestant guessed the wrong amount, the hiker would fall off his papier mâché mountain and the game would be over. Yodel-Ay-Hee-Hoo, we'd certainly be in unknown financial territory at the pharmacy.

"How does a preventative inhaler work?" I wanted to know.

"You'll be inhaling a steroid that will stay localized in your lungs. We want to make your respiratory system less reactive. Do you have an asthma specialist?"

That was like asking if I had a sommelier or a solid gold car at home. "No," I said sheepishly.

"We can give you some recommendations," he replied. "Do you have any questions?"

"What caused this?" I asked. "It's never been this bad before."

"You caught a yucky virus. The inflammation in your lungs has likely been building, and together they caused a problem. Things should improve with the right medications, though."

I nodded. "Thank you very much. I'm feeling a lot better."

"You're welcome. Now, let me get these discharge papers signed, and we'll send you home. I want you to take it easy for a few days. Give your new medications time to work. Don't hesitate to come back to the ER if you're still having trouble, ok? Do you have any more questions?"

"Yeah," said Mom. "Do you have the winning lottery numbers?"

The doctor smiled mildly. Hopefully, he would be as adept at prescribing cheap drugs as he was practicing medicine.

A few minutes later, the nurse came back a final time

with my prescriptions and instructions. She listened to my lungs, which were now crackle-free, and checked my pulse ox, which had returned to normal. Thank God and the miracle of science.

Mom brought the car around while I waited with Sissy. We were all exhausted, and we still had to drive to a 24-hour pharmacy to get my medication. I needed to start my expectorant and antibiotics right away.

The total at Walgreens was over a hundred dollars. Mom muttered a resigned "*Shit*," but said nothing else. I felt like a dog who'd chased a skunk and ended up in a tomato juice bath. I was ashamed but unable to go against my nature. I couldn't help growing up with asthma or a threadbare safety net.

Back home at last, I changed into fresh PJs and returned to the couch. Mom promised to wake me in time to take my first round of steroids and new inhaler. I turned the TV to an infomercial for the noise, and prayed I'd get a good night's sleep.

Before I knew it, sunshine was pouring through the living room windows, and Mom was nudging me awake.

～

I FELT WELL ENOUGH to go to Mammaw's house on Christmas Eve. My late father's side of the family was huge, and once you threw in cousins, great-grandbabies, a half-dozen guitars and a drum set into her modest home on Island Home Avenue, any occasion became a can't-miss party.

Daddy had died in late December during my first year of middle school, forever sullying the Christmas holiday. This didn't stop me from trying to revive it. Each subsequent celebration seemed to get a little easier, partly due to our improving finances and partly due to determination, as I made it my mission to wish all the world a cheerful season's greetings through a gritted-teeth smile.

I still needed to take it easy. Once at Mammaw's, I helped myself to a paper plate loaded with sweet meatballs, fudge, and nuts and ladled green party punch into a dainty glass teacup. There were only two kinds of party punch – red fruit-flavored and green fruit-flavored. Both were non-alcoholic and made from a frozen base that was 99% sugar and tasted like it. Despite not containing alcohol, both flavors burned going down, probably due to the copious amounts of artificial dyes saturating each one. Yet, Christmas Eve wasn't complete without gallons of it shining brightly in Mammaw's best punch bowl, slowly eating away at the glaze holding the receptacle together.

I parked myself on the couch, away from the groups of relatives chatting animatedly in both the kitchen and dining room. The only other person in the living room was my Uncle

Kent, almost old enough to retire and ready for it, snoozing soundly with his ballcap over his eyes. I wanted to change the channel. I watched Uncle Kent for a minute in case he was only resting, but his mustache rumbled along his upper lip like a woolly mammoth trying to outrun a hyena. He was asleep.

I flipped through the channels. A newscaster was droning on about Y2K. While I thought it prudent to prepare for its possibility, I didn't think we'd all wake up on January 1, 2000 and see satellites fall out of the sky or get a bill for a million-dollar Blockbuster Video fine. The world's smartest people were taking it very seriously, and that was enough for me. Any hysteria around the subject seemed designed to only benefit newspaper sales and scummy televangelists hawking end-of-the-world prep kits.

The televangelists, and the people they fleeced, irritated me to no end. How many times did these perfectly coiffed grease pots have to get the date of the rapture wrong before their foolish flock stopped sending them money? And if Christians were going to be Hoovered up to Heaven anyway, why would they need any Y2K prep kits? I knew that many televangelists had built their fortunes on the backs of lonely and poor people, and it angered me greatly. While my faith tradition was adamant that violence wasn't the answer, there was nothing sinful in hoping for an exacting Y2K miracle that erased the televangelists' bank accounts but left all others' intact.

I found Ralphie dressed in his pink bunny suit on another channel and left it there. Sissy eventually wandered back from Frances' house, and we finished the movie together while Mom, deep in conversation with her nieces and nephews, hooted in amusement from the kitchen. It had turned out to be a most pleasant celebration.

~

I WOKE UP IN the early hours of December 26th again unable to breathe. The ambulance was called, I returned to the hospital, and the whole process from a few days before was repeated. A different doctor sent me home with a different preventative inhaler, one he thought would work better. The new inhaler cost an additional eighty dollars.

Scheduling an appointment with an asthma specialist was more difficult since it was the end of the year, and everyone was on vacation. We finally secured a time right before I was to head back to Kentucky, which was still almost two weeks away.

The congestion in my lungs was stubborn, and the steroids in my blister pack and new inhaler kept me wired and anxious. I spent my days with my head over a pot breathing steam and my evenings playing endless rounds of gin rummy with Mom.

Nothing prepared me for the panic. After my first trip to the ER, I assumed I was improving. As long as I took it easy and followed the directions on my prescriptions, I would get better and leave this nightmare behind.

My naiveté in the matter was quite precious. At least once a night, I would wake up gasping for air, my heart pounding as if I'd outrun a serial killer. Sometimes my startled wakings would correspond with nightmares, but often they did not. I would squirt my rescue medication into my lungs, inhaling as deeply as I could without coughing and waking the whole trailer. The albuterol helped, and overall, I was using less than my prescribed limit.

Why weren't the medications working as expected? Thoughts of death and permanent disability began to keep me from falling asleep. I feared the concept I'd had of my own health had been a fantastical delusion, a fragile house of cards that tumbled to the ground with the first stiff breeze of autumn. I delayed my bedtime later each night until I was still watching old black-and-white movies and infomercials at dawn.

A thousand dark things stood between me and 6:00 a.m. Once the rest of the family had gone to sleep, the morning seemed as far away as the shore halfway through a long sea voyage. Without wellness, nothing else mattered. Who gave a crap about acting or pretty clothes or having a boyfriend if my body couldn't be trusted to return to normal after a cruise ship-sized level of medical intervention?

If I couldn't breathe, I couldn't go to school. If I didn't graduate, I'd never get a good job. If I spent my life working below my potential with low energy and no nest egg, I'd languish right above the poverty line until Mom, my perpetual roommate, died. Then I'd join the rest of the working poor under it.

Fear was its strongest and dreams their most precarious in the middle of the night. If I focused on my breathing too much, I'd start to hyperventilate, which would make my hands tingle, adding to the panic. If I tried to go to sleep early, my brain would send a foghorn of imprecise alarm through my body and jolt me awake. After hours of affliction and cycles of anxiety, I'd hear Mom stir in her bedroom, and I could finally rest. Sometimes, if my eyes were closed, Mom would stand by the couch and watch my breathing, like she did when I was a baby. I was too embarrassed to thank her.

Slowly, I inched toward recovery. On New Year's Eve, the three of us threw on casual clothes and headed to a relative's house for a low-key celebration. Nothing weird happened when the clock struck midnight. Eggheads everywhere surely breathed a sigh of relief. I hoped this was a portent of what the year 2000 would bring: the ability to keep moving forward unscathed, even if there was a lot of agitation leading up to it.

I had my answer a few days later when I once again returned to the ER. This time, I endured a contrast IV to check for pulmonary embolisms. The scan was clear, and I was grateful, but I could no longer tell the difference between a genuine asthma attack and whatever was causing the repeated tidal waves of panic. Some of my symptoms were likely due to anxiety, since the expectorants and steroids had finally evicted the grossest slime from my lungs. No amount of anxiety could outwit the doctors, however, who still heard wheezing in their stethoscopes when examining me.

After another long night in the Emergency Department, I was discharged without any medication changes and urged to keep my upcoming specialist's appointment.

"Of course I'll be there!" I'd said with as much pep as I could muster. I felt lower than a hobo drinking stolen hooch under the Gay Street Bridge. The redundant sheaf of privacy notices and hospital payment options clutched in my fist, the third batch in a month, reminded me for the millionth time that so much of life's trajectory hung not on raw talent or learnable skill but on the ability to afford one's own defective humanity. The cost of new prescriptions alone had been enough to defer Santa's visit for our family until next Christmas. I'd not received a single ER bill — yet.

I returned to the waiting room. Mom, Sissy, and Sissy's good friend Miller were huddled together on a row of gray plastic seats, necks contorted and legs stretched in varying stages of sleepiness.

"I'm done," I said. "We can go home now." I looked at Miller. "What are you doing here? You must be terribly bored."

"I'm keeping your sister company," he replied. Miller came off as a quirky know-it-all, but those who looked past his persnickety standards of everything and everyone discovered a most tender heart inside his chest. He was the type who'd help his friends with literally anything, as long as they promised to shut up about it already.

Miller handed me a piece of paper. "I drew this for you," he said. "Sorry you've been going through it lately."

"We've *all* been going through it lately," Mom wearily retorted. I'd been around enough hospitals in my life to experience a well-observed phenomenon found only amongst the trashy, which I called Party Time. Converged on every surgical and emergency waiting area at any time, in any location, was a group of unpolished and outspoken family members gathered to support a loved one in their time of need. Often, the assembled family was of humble means, marked by their voluminous printed t-shirts and half-empty Mountain Dew bottles, but not always. Their primary duty was to render encouragement as Meemaw underwent a toe amputation or Cousin Brittni pushed a new Paislee or Brayleigh into the world. However, they also excelled in hogging the seats and making the waiting room smell like pork rinds.

It had never dawned on me until then that Mom should have been my one and only visitor. Why she'd ever woken up Sissy in the middle of the night just for company (who'd then dragged Miller into it, to boot) was astonishing. Wedging oneself into a hard-molded chair for hours was hardly a party. The patient was already languishing; there was no need for anyone else to suffer in solidarity, and certainly no need to line the waiting room coffee table with greasy pizza boxes, like the MRSA-filled buffet thoughtfully provided by Brittni's estranged common-law husband, Cooter.

The shortcomings of my pedigree weighed as heavily as my impending bills. On top of everything else, I had to acknowledge that we were a little bit trashy.

Miller had drawn a picture of me lying on a stretcher next to an ambulance and looking sad. On the other side of the page, he'd sketched a rainbow and happy sunshine as encouragement for the future.

I chuckled at his round and bespectacled depiction. It looked just like me. "Thanks for the reminder," I told Miller. "I know it will get better eventually."

"Everything gets better eventually," he replied, "or we die and then it doesn't matter anymore. So, either way."

"A most accurate and upbeat reminder," I said. "Now let's all go home and sleep."

~

MY SPECIALIST'S APPOINTMENT RAN the gamut from helpful to awful. After taking a thorough history, the doctor, a pleasant, middle-aged man with paternal energy, recommended a test called the methacholine challenge. Although I'd been diagnosed with asthma in kindergarten – without the stupid test — he needed updated data.

Weren't my pages of emergency department records enough? I wanted to ask. I reluctantly agreed because I needed to get my health back on track. I knew I had to give him a chance to exhibit his expertise, but I dreaded it just the same.

The methacholine challenge involved taking a reading of my base lung function, then having me inhale methacholine, a substance known to induce airway restriction in asthmatic patients, then testing my lung function again. If I truly had asthma, my second lung function score would decrease.

To test my lung function, I exhaled as long and as hard as I could into a handheld device. An attached screen showed several animated lit birthday candles, and my goal was to blow out as many as I could in one breath. I extinguished all but one, which earned praise from the technician.

I inhaled the methacholine after a few minutes of rest. Almost instantly, my chest felt heavier, like I'd added Jayne Mansfield's bra to my own. I took the second lung function test. This time, only half the candles were snuffed out.

"You definitely have asthma," the technician said, with rescue inhaler in hand.

No duh, I thought to myself, as I took a shot of albuterol.

The doctor decided to keep me on the second preventative inhaler prescribed at the emergency room and instructed me to rinse out my mouth after I used it to prevent thrush. *Thrush* was a totally disgusting word, second only to *pustule.* There was no way I'd forget to rinse.

"I want to give you something else," he said. He handed me a gray rectangular object, not quite a foot long, with a removable cover. "This is called a peak flow meter."

I popped open the bottom and observed a mouthpiece printed with a grided scale.

"If you're worried about whether you're having a panic attack or an asthma attack, this is a good tool to help you decide." The doctor took it from me and pushed some plastic markers in place along the side of the grid. He pointed to the green one.

"When your reading is here or above, your asthma is likely well-controlled, and you might be having a panic attack." He pointed to the yellow marker. "If it's here, use your albuterol and check again in a few minutes. If your reading is in the red, you need to go to the ER. It's not a panic attack."

A deluge of relief and gratitude cascaded over me. Is this all it would take to soothe my frazzled mind? A plastic report card? This pleased the anxious, overachieving part of me. I'd *always* been good at report cards, except for those couple of semesters at UT.

"So, if my reading is in the green, but I feel like I can't breathe, I'm just having a panic attack?" I asked for confirmation.

"Of course, if you're having sustained trouble, you should still get checked out. But overall — yes. Your medicines are doing a good job controlling your asthma. The virus you're recovering from is just making it harder to bounce back. You've been through a lot in the last few weeks, and your body is reacting to it."

"But I'm going to be ok?"

"You're going to be ok."

I exited the office and returned to my car, pulling my turtleneck over my nose and mouth to warm the air I was breathing. Nothing made my lungs twitchier than cold winter wind. I'd received good news today. Starting now, I was going to take better care of myself. The last month had been horrible. I'd been deep enough in the hole to taste the dirt being shoveled from above, and I didn't wish to return.

I fastened my seatbelt and started the engine. The Bearden branch of the Knox County Library was a short drive away from my new doctor. I wondered if they had any books about panic attacks. I was determined to send those little gremlins packing, too.

My chest abruptly contracted, and a strained exhale popped out with a whine. I grabbed my peak flow meter and fumbled it open. I tested my breathing in abject terror, hands and scalp tingling.

The meter showed green.

I tried to recenter myself. This was going to be a long year. Possibly, a long century. Did we truly escape Y2K, or would the damage lie latent, slowly rotting our foundations over time?

I recapped the device and returned it to my purse. It was too soon to prognosticate. All I could do was focus on today. The next hour. The next minute. Build tiny victory upon tiny victory until I was back to normal.

My hand flew back into my purse and again grabbed my meter. Most people wouldn't think a plastic doodad was worthy of celebration, but they hadn't rung in the new year with me. There was a certain ceremonial gravitas imbued in my acquirement of this medical noisemaker, and I would treat it as such.

I blew into the device once more, just to check. Green.
Luckily, it was only panic.

TO FLEE OR NOT TO FLEE

I sat quietly in class, surrounded by students on all sides and trying desperately to pay attention to the instructor. Unfortunately, the cycle of panic had already begun; it could not be stopped, only endured.

As long as I was deeply focused on anything but my breathing, I was ok. The moment I became aware of my pattern of inhalation and exhalation, however, the panic would attack viciously. A cascade of symptoms would follow it: deep sighs as I fought air hunger, tingling hands, electric body shocks that originated from the center of my chest. I'd check my peak flow, find it to be normal, and then often take a puff of albuterol just to be safe.

This cycle had repeated itself multiple times a day since I'd returned to Cumberland three weeks ago. Nothing seemed to get rid of it. I thought if I could re-establish a routine and devote my time to studying and theatre, whatever part of my brain responsible for permanently switching me into fight-or-flight mode would eventually get hip to the idea that I was truly ok, and I could move on with life after the destructive health storm of Christmas holiday.

The panic was relentless; it stalked me in acting class, where we were learning stage combat, in the cool and calm library, even when I was in the dining hall eating a bowlful of vanilla soft serve sprinkled with Fruity Pebbles (truly the best topping of all time). All I had to do was accidentally focus on my breathing for a microsecond, and we were off to the races. The panic didn't care how embarrassing or inconvenient its visit was — it showed up louder and faster than a first-date diarrhea fart after a bad appetizer.

As my breathing quickened, I squeezed my *baguette* inconspicuously, trying to redirect my attention. I squeezed my earlobe and elbow fat as well, varying the sensations. I twisted my bangs around my finger and crossed and uncrossed my toes. Nothing was working, as usual. The wave of panic crested with a slam inside my ribcage as my heart skipped a beat and then regulated, forcing an exhale from my lungs and igniting every nerve in terror.

I grabbed my peak flow meter from my backpack and tried to exit as quietly as possible. Did my classmates know something was wrong? My conspicuousness was humiliating.

Outside the classroom, I tested and retested my

breathing. The meter showed green. I walked up and down the hallway until I thought I'd recovered enough to return. Once back inside, I sat staring at the instructor, white knuckles grasping the corners of the desk, concentrating not on taking notes but only on making it through the last fifteen minutes.

When she dismissed us, I left the Bennett Building as fast as I could. I walked through the busiest part of campus quickly, until I was finally off Walnut Street and could cry in peace.

∼

MOM AND SISSY SPENT several hours helping me move back in after Dylan's graduation. We'd made an event out of it, raiding Walmart for fresh shampoo and other incidentals needed for the new semester, then swinging by Arby's for curly fries and sandwiches. After lunch, which Mom insisted on eating inside the restaurant as to not drip Beef-N-Cheddar on the seats of her newish teal Chevy Corsica, we turned my TV to a rerun and started rearranging.

Dylan and I had previously arranged our twin beds on either side of the room, matched by chests of drawers on opposite sides. I decided to flip the whole design around, removing Dylan's bed and moving mine to the middle.

We found an RA who gave us permission to remove the

extra bed, and afterwards, I was left with two desks and two chests. I wanted all four of these pieces. One of the desks could be used as a vanity, the other for studying — and I had more than enough junk to fill up the second chest.

I decided I wanted to move Dylan's chest of drawers next to mine, to create the illusion of a bigger dresser.

"Sissy, come get the corner of this chest. I want to move it beside the other one."

She complied and grabbed the top. We lifted it with a grunt and duckwalked it to the other side of the room. Once in place, I turned to retrieve the vacuum and noticed a pale, broken-off stick lying on the floor.

I went to pick it up and then shrieked.

"IT'S ASLAN!" I howled.

Aslan, Dylan's goldfish who had disappeared from his bowl back in December, lay white and still on the ground. His unseeing eye stared up at me accusingly.

Mom, who'd been cleaning the bathroom, heard me yell and came running. Sissy and I stood over the tiny corpse in disbelief.

"What the hell is that?" Mom asked.

"It's Dylan's fish, Aslan!" I exclaimed sadly. "He jumped out of his bowl at the end of last semester. We pulled the room apart looking for him. We even moved all the furniture. He was nowhere to be found."

"Well, at least you didn't squash him," Mom said. "Poor little fish stick."

"Suffocation is worse, I think," I gulped. "We need to get rid of him. Would somebody else please pick him up? I can't handle it."

Mom bent down and scooped up Aslan with her bare hand.

"Oh my God. *Mom!*" I fussed. "At least use a tissue."

"My first job was plucking feathers off dead chickens in Pine Bluff, Arkansas," she said, unaffected. "'Ain't nothin' nastier than that."

She took the goldfish to the bathroom, flipped up the toilet lid, and tossed it in.

I did the honors, flushing Aslan's remains into the sewer system of Williamsburg, Kentucky, where he would eventually bob and weave down the peaceful Cumberland River forever. It was moving, in a way.

"Please wash your hands," I implored. "You can even use my new soap."

Mom stepped over to the sink and started lathering. I glanced down into the toilet bowl and recoiled.

"Oh, my Lord," I said, clutching my shirt. *"He didn't flush."*

Aslan continued to float, circling the top of the water tail first.

I immediately pushed the handle again and watched the

toilet try to take down the remnants. The fish's body was obstinate; it remained even after a second flush.

"This is totally disgusting!" I said. "He's like, petrified or something."

In the same way I could look back over my life and find instances where a benevolent God rescued my family from catastrophe, instances of the opposite were ten times as prevalent. There seemed to exist in the universe a class of supernatural assholes created only to cause annoyance, strife, and pain. How many times had each of us climbed the heights of victory only to suffer a badly timed flat tire or news of a devastating illness the same day? Just when we got the promotion or finally paid off the credit card, here came the slick shower floor to knock out a tooth or a storm to blow the roof off our house. These goblins were everywhere, waiting to choke us on leftover Oreo crumbs after a delicious dinner.

I'd returned to school mentally hanging by a thread. I was convinced the driftwood leftovers in the toilet were a sign, and not a good one.

"Do you want me to try peeing on it?" asked Mom.

"No!" I cried.

We had to try something, though. Mom wandered into the common area on the hunt. She finally picked up her paper Arby's cup and brought it back into the bathroom.

After taking the last swig of sweet tea from the container, she dumped the ice into the sink and filled up the cup with water.

She poured the water directly on top of Aslan as she flushed again. This time, the extra force from above pushed him out of the bowl, and he disappeared from sight.

"Are you going to call Dylan and tell her what happened?" Mom asked.

"Absolutely *not*," I replied. "I'll go to my grave with this very weird secret."

Once we'd moved Aslan's dresser next to the other one, the move-in was complete. I still had clothes to fold, but Mom and Sissy had done all they could.

"We're gonna get on the road, Punkinhead," Mom announced. "Do you have your new medication?"

"Yeah, I'm good. Thank you for the help," I said, hugging them both. "I'm glad to be here, but you know I'll miss y'all. I'll be back in the bushes outside the trailer before you know it."

"Ha ha," Mama said sarcastically. "If I catch you at home this weekend, we're eating nothing but Tuna Helper."

∼

THE DINING HALL WAS open from 4:30 to 7:30 each evening. I usually ate early because of rehearsal. Auditions for our next performance were yet to be held, and I was already waiting outside at 4:25, hopping impatiently from foot to foot. The anxiety hadn't let up since class. I was hoping the noise and good smells inside would finally short-circuit the cycle so I could have some relief.

My mind felt furry as I pushed my tray through the line. I chose my supper based on how distracting it might be. Soup was good, if it was hot enough to burn my tongue. I passed up the soft rolls for a crunchy piece of French bread dotted with sesame seeds. I skipped the milk, not wanting to add snottiness to my list of complaints, and sat down to eat.

Carlene and Danielle joined me a few minutes later.

"How's it going?" Danielle asked.

"Pretty crappy," I told her. "My panic attacks are getting worse. This one started three hours ago." As soon as I mentioned it, the air whooshed from my lungs and I doubled over, trying to catch my breath.

"Are you ok?" said Carlene with concern.

The dining hall was packed with far more students than had been in class, upping the embarrassment quotient by a factor of five. I puffed into my peak flow meter anyway. It showed green.

"I'm fine," I replied, resting my chest on my knees. "I mean, I'm not having an asthma attack. My mind just won't cooperate."

I chewed heavily on a bite of bread, tapping my foot in

distraction so I could swallow more easily. I tasted the soup and then had a sip of ice water. I managed to finish my meal by alternating the items with no breaks in between.

Carlene watched me skeptically. "Are you sure you're ok? Maybe you should get checked out."

"The student health center is already closed for the day," I said.

"If it's been like this for hours, maybe you should go to the ER. They can check for sure to see if it's your asthma. If it's not, they can give you something to relax."

The feeling of defeat was enormous. She was right. I needed help. I hadn't recovered, even after a month of rest and doctors.

I still didn't want to go. "The closest hospital is that tiny *Hee Haw* nightmare in Jellico. No, thank you."

"Yeah, that place is scary," added Danielle. "It's right across the street from their funeral home."

"You could go up to London. That one's ... better," said Carlene.

I was experiencing the biggest drawback of attending college in the middle of nowhere - in case of an emergency, you were screwed. Tiny rural hospitals were better than nothing, but that was a low bar to clear in an area still dotted with outhouses.

"Even if I wanted to go, I'm in no shape to drive."

"I can drive your car," offered Carlene.

"I know that song," Danielle interjected. "Neer neer neer neer, neer NEER neer-neer neer neer," she sang.

"You don't mind sitting at the ER forever? Are you sure?"

Carlene shrugged. "Hey babe – the biggest event in my hometown is the Fourth of July tractor pull. It doesn't take much to get me excited."

"I'll go, too," said Danielle. "Anything's better than writing a paper."

"Thanks, guys," I said with affection. I almost felt tears prick my eyes, but instead my lungs forced another exhale, and my fingertips began to tingle. I was making the right decision.

～

LONDON WAS A SMALL town like Corbin, both approximately a twenty-minute drive north of Cumberland College. If Corbin was a one-horse town, London might have had two, owing only to the hospital.

We sat alone in the waiting room save for a wiry man with ragged facial hair who kept his eyes closed and let out a moan of pain every couple of minutes, like clockwork. I assumed he was truly in pain but also addicted to whatever substance was cheap and easy to score around London. Drugs were a goddamned scourge. Growing up in an extended family poisoned by alcoholism killed any appetite I'd ever had to experiment or throw caution to the wind during a raging party. In my experience, the people most susceptible to addiction had the most reasons to start using and therefore the most to lose when they were inevitably destroyed by it. I wanted nothing to do with any social group that minimized these risks in the name of recreation.

The nurse called my name, and I followed her past a folding door and into an adequate but drab room.

"What brings you here today?" she asked briskly.

I explained my history as quickly as possible and told her that I wasn't sure if I was having an asthma attack or a never-ending panic attack.

I initially thought her conciseness was part of an efficient personality, but as she scribbled only a few notes onto a clipboard without making eye contact or asking any follow-up questions, I knew she'd pigeonholed me into the same drug-seeking category as the fellow waiting outside.

A bolt of anger thundered through the panic, and I briefly felt camaraderie with the man in the waiting room. The truth was, if I could have swallowed a pill that made my hands stop tingling and heart stop palpitating long enough to catch up on homework, I would have taken it, even if it came out of someone's dirty jeans pocket. In that moment, my misery was greater than my resolve.

The nurse checked my pulse ox, which was normal, and took my blood pressure. A doctor came in to examine me immediately after she left. If nothing else, their speed was impressive.

The doctor was kinder than the nurse. I again explained my history. He listened to my lungs. "I don't hear anything that concerns me," he said. "We could give you a breathing treatment, but I don't think you need one. Sounds like panic attacks to me."

"That's ... good, I guess?" I acknowledged. "I mean, I'm grateful it's not asthma." I pressed my fingertips against my eyelids. "I feel wretched all the time, though." I began to cry.

"Do you have a doctor back home?"

"I have two."

"I think you need to talk to them about prescribing a medication that can help with anxiety. You don't have to suffer."

The idea of onboarding another new medication overwhelmed me. At this rate, I'd need five work-study jobs to afford them all.

"I'm going to give you something to help you relax tonight and then discharge you. Make an appointment with your doctor, ok?"

"Ok," I answered. "Thank you."

The nurse returned holding a small metal tray with a syringe placed in the center.

A shot? I wanted to ask her. *Is that necessary? Couldn't I just swallow the pill in front of you?*

Then again, her attitude made me want to throw up. Better safe than sorry. I pulled up the sleeve of my shirt with a sigh.

"No," she said. "I have to administer this injection into your upper hip."

She was enjoying this, I could tell.

I climbed off the table and unbuttoned my jeans. "Fine," I said.

It was childish, but I tugged my jeans all the way down and exposed my full buttocks to her.

"Here ya go."

Her aim was true. She threw the needle into my upper hip as cleanly and forcefully as the cruelest health department nurse twelve hours into an eight-hour shift. I fought the effort to react in pain.

"You should start to feel more relaxed soon," said the nurse. "I'll go prepare your discharge papers."

I wanted to suggest a more internal reciprocal injection, sideways. Instead, I smiled sweetly.

"Thank you. I do appreciate your help today."

By the time Carlene got back on the interstate, I was feeling the effects of the shot. The world seemed suddenly full of good people, and I wanted to hug every tree and sign we passed simply in acknowledgement of their existence. I felt sleepy and ravenously hungry.

"Can we stop by a drive-thru?" I asked Carlene.

"It's your car," she replied.

"Frosties for everybody, then!" I sloshed happily.

"Sounds like you're feeling better," Danielle said.

"This is the best I've been in weeks," I told her. "I might actually sleep tonight."

"In that case," added Danielle, "I'll take some fries, too."

I stumbled back into my room a while later with a bacon cheeseburger and fries of my own. While there was no doubt I was feeling calmer, my thinking was slow, and I knew this kind of short-acting drug wasn't a long-term solution. I prayed it would reset my system for a few days until I could talk to Mom about going back to the doctor.

I took a bite of my burger and observed as my brain labeled each taste sensation. The bun had the sweet but metallic smell of a commercial bakery. The bacon was oozingly crisp and dirty from the leftover drippings on the grill. Exquisite. I felt as though I was watching a movie of my taste buds describing their experience to my frontal cortex.

I took another bite, this one rich with ketchup. Ketchup had a slightly rough texture I'd never noticed before, filaments of pulped tomato swirled into a deliciously salty galaxy. What a beautiful condiment.

I looked at the burger, then the yellow concrete walls of my dorm room, then the burger again.

"Am I stoned?" I asked aloud.

Luckily, the burger said nothing.

I decided I'd eaten enough. I flipped over on my side – the one the nurse hadn't played darts on – and closed my eyes to sleep.

RELIEF LASTED EXACTLY THIRTY-FIVE hours. I had one normal day but then overslept the morning after and missed my opportunity to stop by the dining hall for breakfast. I grabbed a box of cookies and some pretzels I'd purchased as snacks and sat down quickly to eat.

The cookies were dry and barely flavored, cheap souvenirs left over from my and Sissy's latest weekend jaunt to Big Lots. I popped a whole one into my mouth and my throat seized, turning the cookie to sawdust. I couldn't swallow. My heart started the familiar gallop associated with a panic attack. I stood over the trash can and spit the half-chewed cookie into it.

I was livid. Why couldn't my body just *behave?* I slapped my open palm hard against the wall, wishing it was my face. Why did every success in my life come packaged with an evil twin? I'd wrestled with poverty and body shame since childhood. The moment I'd gotten close to resolving either of them, a physiological ghoul set up residence in my brain, daring me to prosper.

Things could always be worse, I told myself, and my body reacted with an exhaled lung whoosh so snappishly pitiless, I fell to my knees breathlessly. Yes, it could always be worse, like it was and ever had been for billions of humans since the beginning of time.

Wound without end, amen.

I thought my mind would break apart from the grief of it all. I wasn't special. The world would go on without me the second I died, which didn't have to be when I was old. My death might be painless and quick, if I fell asleep one day in my recliner and woke up in Heaven, or it might be undignified and cruel, body wasting away in a nursing home bed as my brain powered down what was left of a once formidable structure.

Even when God delivered miracles, there was no promise that our final days would be any better than the worst ones we'd survived. This seemed like horribly unfair treatment from a loving God. Christianity's clanging dissonance on the matter was one of the biggest reasons I kept one foot on the dock of secularism even as the other foot longed to follow Jesus, which did nothing but pin me in place like a biology class frog.

Secular or religious, humans were nothing but a bunch of superstitious troglodytes. Most of us would never respect the inevitability of death. True to our egotistical nature, we'd never appease but instead try to outsmart it with exercise and Sudoku and the inflated assurance of "good genes." The fact that a person could run marathons, eat only organic foods, and still die early from being hit by a car proved that anything we did to outrun the Grim Reaper was ultimately futile. Staying a few inches ahead of its outstretched bony digits was the best we could hope for.

I crouched on the floor in tears. Jesus warned His followers to expect trouble in the world, yet I needed more from Him than just a heads up.

My first class was almost halfway finished by the time I stopped crying. I'd be worthless there, anyway. I knew what I had to do.

I spent the time until lunch walking up and down the carpeted hall in front of our suite. On one end was a wall, on the other a door that led to the sidewalk. Any normal person would have spent the time breathing fresh air, maybe going to the library or bookstore for distraction. I had a head stuffed full of trauma, sadly. The outside world was now nothing but a place to showcase debilitating panic attacks. This was not the kind of public attention I sought.

Lunch was ok. I went at a different time than I

usually met my friends and sat alone with some lasagna and peas – mushy foods that wouldn't choke me if my throat seized up again. The afternoon sun filled the dining hall, outlining the students with a golden haze. Some of their heads were kissed with it, like halos, and the pleasant tableau made me recall the picture-perfect visit I'd made with Mom years ago to tour Cumberland's campus.

I was going to miss this place.

Back inside my room, I stared out the window, thinking. The view was spectacularly ugly – a thick gray retaining wall with an alley cut-through – but I'd always appreciated it since it meant I could change shirts without bothering to close the curtains. No one had been down the alley in two and a half years except a lone motorcyclist, and I'd ducked just in time to avoid giving him an eyeful.

Finally, it was four o'clock. Mom's schedule as a lunchlady hadn't changed in a decade, so unless she'd decided to go 'scooterpoopin' — her name for errands – after work, I knew she'd been home for ten minutes, long enough to change her clothes and let Cookie outside.

Mom picked up on the second ring. "Hello?" she said suspiciously.

She knew. She *knew*.

"It's me."

"Pooh, is everything ok?"

"I'm ok," I said through tears. "I had to go to the emergency room the day before yesterday for a bad panic attack."

She didn't reply so I continued. "The ER doctor gave me a shot to calm down. It only helped for a day. That's it. He wants me to talk to Dr. Lithgow about anxiety meds. The past three weeks have been *horrible*."

Emotionally, she and I had remained as close as when I wore the umbilical cord. I could tell by the cadence of her breathing that her focus was far away — not due to exasperation but instead in preparation.

"What do you want to do?" she asked after a few moments.

My dam of resolve, bulging and leaking since the end of last semester, crumbled into smithereens. Defeat swept away what was left of my pride.

"I want to come home, Mama," I sobbed.

"I said to myself, 'It's too early to send her back to school. She needs to stay here for a while,'" Mom fretted. "You were so pale. When Sissy and I left the dorm, I almost cried myself."

There was so much to do before Mom shuttled me back to Knoxville to convalesce. "I'm going to have to find out how to withdraw this semester. I won't screw it up like I did at UT."

"Honey, I'm so sorry," Mom said.

Friends, acting, academics – all put on hold indefinitely.

My success story, just out of reach once more. I'd be fifty years old before I graduated college.

I didn't have enough grit left to feel anything but relief. Embarrassing, shameful relief. The poor little baby bird who still couldn't get her act together would be back under Mama's wing in no time.

Thank God, I thought. I needed to heal, and at least I had a place to do so.

"Thank you," I replied, certain she'd understand that my gratitude extended well past the polite acknowledgement of what she'd said.

"Can you make it until Friday?" she asked. "I'll drive up then to move you out."

"I guess."

"Ok, Heather Pooh. I love you."

"Love you." I hung up the phone and waited for my suite-mates to return from class. I sat on the common room couch scribbling plans until then.

"I need to tell you guys something," I began, barely giving them a chance to get in the door.

"What's up?" asked Ana.

"It's no secret that I've had a terrible few weeks. After talking to my mom, I decided to go back home for a while."

They were shocked. "What?" exclaimed Carlene. "No! Please don't go."

Danielle started singing New Kids on the Block's "Please Don't Go Girl" to me, using her water bottle as a microphone. "Aww, man," she added. "Well, that stinks."

"What did your Mom say?" asked Ana.

"She said that when she dropped me off at the beginning of the semester, she knew I wasn't better yet. She's coming to move me home Friday."

"So soon, gordita?"

"As soon as Admissions processes everything, there's no need to stick around. I'm not going back to class. There's no point."

"Are you *sure?*" Carlene wanted to know.

"I'm sure that I don't want to leave, and just as sure that I have to. If I've got to start taking anxiety medications *and* get used to my new asthma ones, I'll be lucky to fall asleep by dawn each day. I'm embarrassingly high-strung. I don't want to go, though. I'm really going to miss you all."

I paused, feeling tears pool in my eyes. "A lot."

"So go home and get better," said Danielle. "You can come back next semester. We'll save you a hard and uncomfortable bed."

I was too sad to laugh, but her joke made me crack a smile. "Ok, deal."

"You better not sneak out of here without saying bye," warned Carlene.

"Don't worry," I said. "You've all met my mother. She's about as inconspicuous as a marching band. The whole campus will know I'm leaving."

~

BREAKING THE NEWS OF my departure to Tex and my fellow actors was oddly painless. Even though everyone said the right things, I didn't get emotional when I hugged them goodbye. I feared it was disassociation. Theatre was the best part of college, save for my friends, and I'd just bought a one-way ticket home. I felt so numb, it barely registered to learn I was leaving right before the opening of the beautiful new Fine Arts center.

The folks in Admissions were kind and made sure I withdrew appropriately so I could return. As it stood, my first student loan payment would be due in ninety days, unless I qualified for a hardship program.

I gave myself a headache thinking about the realities of an incomplete education. I'd probably qualify for a hardship program – I'd been the poster child for government assistance since kindergarten, when we'd lived in the projects for the first time – but I desperately wanted to graduate. The space between today and graduation was an unknowable chasm, though, and my most important job was to heal.

On Friday morning, I didn't leave my room. I listened to

my suitemates get ready as usual, then gathered my essentials from the bathroom after they'd left for class. Ironically, I'd had fewer panic attacks since my conversation with Mom. My decision to leave school was the right one. As I sat alone eating leftover generic sour cream and onion chips for breakfast because I was too sorrowful to make it to the dining hall, I was reminded that 'easy' and 'right' seldom aligned.

I watched TV until I heard a knock at the suite door. Mom was here.

"Hey woman, it's me!" she shouted from the other side. "We're here to help you move!"

Who's 'we?' I wondered. Sissy was exempt from this excursion. It was a school day, and she was in class.

I opened the door. Beside Mom stood Davy, my ex-boyfriend, whom I'd not spoken with since our breakup. He and Mom still attended the same church, best buds despite a clear conflict of interest.

I fought the urge to slam it shut and hurl myself through the bedroom window, screaming all the way.

"Well ... hi," I said to both of them. After Mom kissed my cheek, Davy and I shared a brief and awkward hug. What was he doing here?

"I hope you don't mind me tagging along," Davy said, reading my mind. "Your Mom said the TV was really heavy and she didn't think the two of you could lift it."

Sissy, with the help of a few well-placed curse words, had hauled the TV into the dorm by herself a few weeks ago. Whatever reason Mom had given Davy was an excuse. She'd wanted company on the ride up, and that was it. For all her protective instincts, Mom sometimes exhibited a selfish myopia that cut to the quick, like the time in fifth grade she'd wanted me, not her, to tell my Awana teacher we were too poor to afford the uniforms. She thought it would teach fearlessness. Instead, I'd quit Awanas to avoid being humiliated.

I couldn't keep quiet about this. "That is very kind," I replied. "I'll unplug it, and you can go ahead and take it to the car."

Davy respectfully grabbed the molded hand grips on the back of the television and hoisted it off the chest, peeking around the side to see where he was going. I took Mom's keys from her purse and stuffed them into Davy's pocket as he made his way out of the suite.

The words left my mouth the second the door closed behind him.

"What in the actual hell is he doing here?"

Mom reacted the same way any time she knew she'd made a mistake, with an irritated, "Oh!" and a sound of exasperation that was like a raspberry and a scoff all at once.

"I didn't think you'd mind, Heather Pooh. He knows you're having a tough time."

"I sure am, and you thought the person I needed to see most besides you, in my weakened and bedraggled state, was my ex-boyfriend with whom I haven't talked in six months?"

"We can't lift that TV!"

"First of all, yes, we could. Second, I would rather leave it here than be forced to make small talk for ninety minutes while we celebrate my double drop-out from college — which must be some kind of record, by the way — with my ex. It's too late now, though."

"I'm sorry," Mom said quietly. "What do you want me to do?"

"Nothing *now*. We can't have him hitchhike back to Knoxville. I'll live. I guess."

My suitemates trickled in as Mom, Davy, and I made trips to the car to load the rest of my belongings. The Corsica was packed tight, especially with the addition of a former romantic interloper.

I couldn't put it off any longer. It was time to say goodbye.

"Ladies, I'm gonna miss you," I said, hugging Danielle, Ana, and Carlene in turn. I sniffed sadly as I crushed my face into theirs.

"You'll be back," said Ana with a warm smile.

"Well, of course she'll be back," interjected Mom gregariously. "I already told her that if she didn't, I'll take her place up here and *she* can be the lunchlady."

They giggled politely. Everyone adored Mom for the first fifteen minutes. Only people who truly loved her lasted longer than that. I would try to remind myself of that fact when I was forced into an extended chat with my ex-boyfriend on one of the worst days of my life.

Mom hugged each of my suitemates and left to find Davy. My things were packed. The battle was over.

"Stay in touch," Carlene told me, "and don't let this crap steal your joy." She pronounced it *joey,* like always, and I bit my lip to keep from crying. I'd only been an hour away from home this whole time, and yet I'd somehow stumbled into a completely different world, full of the very best things.

"Will do." Tears threatened again, and I decided to beat a hasty retreat. I couldn't stay here forever.

"I'll see y'all later, then."

I pulled the heavy suite door closed behind me, and re-markably, it latched softly. The door had a tendency to slam shut and startle the whole floor. I was glad my departure was a gentle one.

I got into the back seat of Mom's car, crowded on one side by the TV. The dark, convex screen faced me, reflecting my facial expressions as we pulled away from Asher Hall.

"Do you want me to drive around so you can see campus one more time?" asked Mom.

Did Napoleon deign to jog the bloody fields near Waterloo as he planned his abdication?

My countenance remained placid. "Hard pass," I said.

A few minutes later, Mom merged onto Interstate 75 South. We'd be back in Knoxville soon enough.

I'd left the University of Tennessee a failure. I was leaving Cumberland College the same way. No one's diploma was stamped *Almost Graduated*.

I leaned against the stiff fabric headrest, no longer in the driver's seat. My surrender was complete. I was being toted back to Mama's trailer the same way my belongings were – wedged anywhere I would fit, jostling against the monstrous TV just like my basket of smelly socks.

A thought flitted across my tattered mind. *Maybe I should've tied a white pair of granny panties to the antenna so that everyone would know my crushing defeat.*

I was surprised to hear myself chuckle.

My friends were right – I'd be back. I wouldn't let this crap steal my *joey*.

"What's so funny back there?" asked Davy.

"Nothing," I replied. "Thinking about laundry."

Huzzah! Huzzah! Let us hail the unconquering queen!

The first step in healing was to admit that one needed to be healed. I'd already done that. Apparently, the next step was to distract oneself with small talk until the next step emerged.

Channeling the theatrical energy that had sustained me for years, I pictured myself draped in ermine, crowned with a glittering coronet heavy with priceless jewels.

With regal bearing, I straightened my posture and put on a pleasant smile for the torturous ride back. Wiser monarchs might have sought counsel, asking for support from advisors and loyal subjects alike as they spent an immoderate amount of time floundering their way back upstream.

However, this royal highness sat upon a throne decoupaged with medical bills and student loan payments, hyperventilating with panic and unsure of the impact of her reign.

"Has anyone seen any good movies?" was the best I could do.

A DRAMATICALLY DIFFERENT TURN OF EVENTS

"Excuse me, honey," asked the petite, frosted blonde grandma. "Is it time for the free gift with purchase?"

I straightened to full height. I'd been bent over the extra stock cabinet, replenishing the lipstick supply for our upcoming event. The staticky cellophane holding the packs together was aggravating, and I took care not to touch the metal parts of the color display.

"No ma'am," I replied. "That starts next Saturday."

The grandma considered my words. She took one hand off her Liz Claiborne purse and rested it on my shoulder. She leaned in conspiratorially. "I'll come back then," she whispered, as if she were the first person to devise such a plan.

"I absolutely *love* that yellow lotion!" she said in farewell, her nylon Alfred Dunner separates swishing noisily as she retreated.

The East Towne Proffitt's Clinique counter would be chaotic during Bonus Time, and we were deep in preparation. Practically every woman in Knoxville would descend upon our brightly lit bay, clamoring for the tiny samples of skincare and fragrance due them with any purchase of $19.50 (or more). Clinique had scores of loyal customers, but Bonus Time brought in hundreds extra. Local newscasters and rural aunts alike would ring our counter like the bloodthirsty patrons of ancient Rome, elbowing each other semi-politely as they fought for our attention.

"Did you hear that, Keke?" I asked my fellow consultant. "Granny's just *gotta* have it ... next week."

Keke curled a finger into the collar of her white uniform, made to resemble a lab coat, and shook it back and forth to fan her neck. "It's going to be wild. I had a whole group stop me in the food court yesterday. You should have seen their faces when I told them Bonus Time hadn't started yet. I thought one lady was going to shank me with her plastic knife."

"Next time, take the Aromatics tester with you. You can use it as mace." Aromatics was one of our most popular fragrances. To me, it smelled like the lair of mean church ladies, the ones who treated their choral solos like *American Idol* auditions and never hesitated to ask the congregation for safe travel prayers before their lavish Caribbean cruises.

This was my second Bonus Time. I'd been working for

Clinique for a year. After leaving Kentucky and recovering on the couch for a month, the medical bills began to pile up, and I needed money. Thankfully, the medication I'd eventually been prescribed to help with anxiety took the edge off my panic attacks. My asthma stabilized as well, and I felt good enough to work. I was also granted temporary forbearance on my student loans that would allow any paychecks to spread further. I hoped to work only long enough to pay off my medical debts and then return to school.

A funny thing had happened, though – I'd stumbled into a grown-up job and found out I was pretty good at it. I'd been obsessed with makeup since my earliest days, armed with 99-cent Wet N'Wild lipsticks since elementary school and forcing Sissy to undergo toothpaste facials to 'open' her pores. My dream growing up was to own a white lacquer vanity stuffed to the brim with every lip goo, blusher, and mascara in production.

The idea of working in cosmetics seemed off-limits to someone like me. In Knoxville, the women behind the counters were neatly attired with impeccable grooming — purebred poodles when it came to looks and bulldogs when it came to meeting sales goals. They were beautiful as well as scary, adept at strong-arming meek customers into treating themselves to liners and glosses when they really only wanted the lipstick, and muscular from repeatedly spritzing perfume on anyone within a fifty-foot radius.

Davy and I had reforged a fragile friendship. One evening, not long after I returned home, I'd accompanied him to West Town Mall, where my future was revealed.

After Davy bought the sweater he'd been looking for, we visited our friend Shannon behind the Clinique counter. Shannon was our high school's former cheer captain, and it showed. She reminded me of Peaches 'N Cream Barbie – fit, blonde, and blessed with a year-round tan. Although Shannon's gorgeous queen bee look was straight out of central casting, she was laid-back and self-deprecating, never taking herself too seriously.

Shannon was leaning against the side of the bay. Her white lab coat dress was creaseless, and her hair was its usual shampoo commercial perfection. Her expression, however, betrayed the elegance of the upscale department store in which she was employed. In fact, I'd seen it a million times before sitting next to her in class.

Shannon was bored. "Hey!" said Davy. "How's it going?"

Her face lit up with interest at the sound of his voice, and she came to life.

"I'm *so* bored," Shannon announced. "I've not had a customer in an hour."

"Isn't this place always busy?" Davy wondered. "Everybody comes to the mall."

"Last week was Bonus Time. We were slammed. I never want to hear the words, 'Is this enough to get my free gift?' ever again."

"Was it that bad?" asked Davy.

"I'm dead inside," Shannon said flatly.

The worst seemed to be over. Standing around looking beautiful and not having to talk to anyone, even some of the time, sounded like a dream job.

"I would give anything to work at a makeup counter," I told her. "There's no way they'd ever hire me, though. The best I've done is TJ Maxx. Did I ever tell you that one time somebody peed in the dressing room during my shift, and I had to clean it up?"

"What?" gasped Davy.

"I know! They didn't even bother to put the clothes they tried on back onto the rack," I sniffed. "Animals."

"*Girl*," said Shannon. "You are more than qualified to work here."

"Really?"

"All you have to do is act like their best friend and be confident in what you're saying. It's not brain surgery. It's just eyeshadow."

"I could do that. At least I could put my acting skills to good use. Are you guys hiring?"

"Not here, but one of the stores will be. Some chick's always getting promoted or married or graduating. You should check it out."

"What the heck. I will," I told Shannon. "I need some kind of job, and fast. What about Bonus Time? Didn't you say it was awful?"

"It is," Shannon agreed, "but it's only twice a year, and you get extra commission. Oh, and you get a ton of free product."

"Speaking of which," said Davy, "do you have any men's skincare you'd like to donate to a good cause? The good cause being my adorable face, of course."

"Sure, Davy Gravy," she said cheerfully. "First, give me a cig. Heather, you can pretend to work here while I run out and smoke it."

～

THE NEXT DAY, I'D called every cosmetics counter in the city asking if they had any openings. East Towne had a few. There were two malls in Knoxville: West Town and East Towne. West Town shoppers were more affluent, but both malls were clean and serviceable. I would be happy working at either of them. Nothing in Knoxville could ever be *that* fancy; a sort of proud Appalachian unfussiness had taken hold a century prior, and no amount of new money or Northern transplants would erase it completely.

I felt more comfortable at East Towne anyway. No matter what Shannon said, I didn't think selling cosmetics would be as easy for me as it was for her. Plenty of women wanted to look like Barbie. They would buy anything slapped on their face, or hers, if they were convinced it would help them snag a Ken of their own. I felt like the funky-limbed, off-brand doll little girls tried to incorporate into their playtime because they felt sorry for it. I was nervous that my sales would be exclusively ones of pity.

Somehow, I got the job. My interview went well, and my résumé was good enough to pass muster. I underplayed my desire to return to college as soon as I was out of debt, which was going to take time no matter what. Soon, I was East Towne Proffitt's new Clinique beauty consultant.

My first week was eye-opening. The commute from our trailer in Karns was long. I had to wake up early to apply a full face of makeup and make sure my lab coat uniform was ironed. Clinique consultants had a certain look because we were selling to a particular customer. Our consultants were fresh-faced with understated makeup. We focused on lab-created skin care and attracted clients with sensitive or troubled areas. Despite never being able to afford anything more extravagant than Noxzema to clean my face, I rarely got blemishes, and my skin was as wrinkle-free as any young person's. This unspoiled canvas was the perfect billboard to show off our products, and it was likely the only reason I'd been hired.

Each brand had their own image. Estée Lauder owned Clinique, but their own consultants were styled elegantly in navy blue dresses, meant to evoke the quiet wealth of an older sister who only visited on Christmas but brought expensive gifts. Lancôme artists wore black to show off their dazzling yet heavy-handed makeup palettes – smoky eyes with plenty of shimmer and Parisian-inspired carmine or magenta lips. Elizabeth Arden's advisors were relegated to frumpy full-body aprons, despite being the business original after which all cosmetics companies modeled themselves; and Clarins was, well, arguably the fanciest line Proffitt's had, since it was expensive and French. Too bad the consultants looked like flight attendants from the 1970s, buttoned tight into red polyester jackets with white pussy-bow blouses spilling from the front and inevitably getting dragged through open containers of product.

Whether we were called consultants, beauty advisors, makeup artists, or skin experts, we all had the same goal: sell the absolute hell out of our respective lines' products and keep those customers coming back for more.

I'd been commuting for a few weeks when I started thinking about finding a place of my own. I hadn't come close to paying off my medical bills, yet Mom was getting edgy about me living at home and not contributing more. I wasn't angry with her – not exactly – but her hunger for better things got stronger the longer I stayed, and whether she realized it or not, she was becoming a barnacle on my already heavily patched rowboat.

Generational poverty was funny that way. I was welcome to stay at home as long as it took to pay off my bills, *if* I'd gotten a fast-food or less glamorous retail job. The minute Mom discovered I was earning a salary comparable to hers, however, the rules were wordlessly modified. Suddenly, I was expected to fork over money towards the utility bill and the lot rent, since in her eyes, I could now afford to. I'd been chipping in since I got my first job and so had Sissy. Sometimes, our money had been the only thing standing between us and an empty refrigerator.

What Mom and countless other broke matriarchs didn't understand was that when fortune shone down upon one of their children, every available tool needed to be deployed to raise our chances of escaping poverty for good. We were miles behind the average middle-class family in opportunities. We couldn't risk getting stuck in the mud or bearing any extra weight that would hurt our chances of leveling the playing field. The most important thing our mothers could do was to keep tending us the best they could and trust that we'd come back to rescue them, not sacrifice us to the same insufficient financial machinations that kept us stuck in the first place.

I knew I'd never leave my mother behind, even if she didn't. Mama was slow to trust anyone because of her own hardscrabble past. I likely wouldn't be able to prove my good intentions for years, and the double-tightrope walk of saving myself while promising a lifeline felt unendurable.

There were practical considerations as well. We'd all outgrown the ratty trailer. At this point, it was only held together by the thinnest coating of liquid nails and layers of stubborn pet hair buttressing the corners. Sissy was now living in the dorms at her college in middle Tennessee – already making better decisions than I ever had — and Mom would likely try to downsize just to have something new, especially if I wasn't there to split the bills.

My makeshift beauty setup at the trailer hadn't changed since seventh grade. My bedroom, although a welcome upgrade from the cramped shared spaces of childhood, was barely big enough for the twin bed, chest of drawers, and side table that doubled as my vanity. My vanity seat was a classy upside-down plastic tub that once held peaches for the Karns cafeteria. At this rate, I'd be crowded out of my room by gratis Clinique products right before the dilapidated walls finally fell down around us. We'd lived life at full throttle here since 1990, and it was obvious.

I checked the *News-Sentinel* classifieds for apartments. I'd already assumed I'd only be able to afford the cheapest places, and I was right. West Knoxville apartments, the ones with community gyms and washer/dryer hookups, were wildly out of my price range. The most affordable listings were in South Knoxville, where we'd lived with Daddy. I should have known a return to South Knoxville was inevitable. I guessed God was giving me a chance to overwrite the devastating exit after his death.

I narrowed my selection to two choices: the Southwood complex on Sevier Avenue or an upstairs apartment in 4th and Gill, Knoxville's most bohemian neighborhood. I invited Mom along to help me decide. We started in 4th and Gill, where Knoxville's highest concentration of creative people lived. I loved the idea of front-porch buskers and free-spirit-ed neighbors who knocked on the door to borrow tempera paint and the devil's lettuce instead of eggs or sugar. The tradeoffs of living in such a desirable area, however, were soon made apparent.

The apartment was located on the top floor of a histor-ic Victorian-style home. The exterior was painted a funky salmon color that was in good shape on the front and peeling on the sun-facing side. Mom and I climbed a rickety interior staircase to access the apartment. At Mom's insistence, we left the landlady in the foyer.

My stomach sunk a little deeper with each stair creak. The house smelled musty and wasn't any nicer than the trailer I was desperate to leave behind. The apartment, if you could call it that, was an open space tucked into what might have been an attic. There was a tiny ancient range dating from what were probably the earliest days of electricity tucked into one corner and a doorless bathroom in the other. The space was mostly covered with chintzy rose wallpaper, except for the bathroom, which was the same bright blue as artificial raspberry candy.

"This isn't ... bad," I said optimistically. "It's a cool neighborhood. I'd get some good exercise climbing those stairs every day."

"Heather," Mom began, "my first job was plucking feathers off dead chickens in Pine Bluff, Arkansas. Their coops were in better shape than this apartment."

She only mentioned the chickens when she wanted to highlight an obvious fact. I hated that she was right.

"I know," I sighed. "I'm just excited to get my own place. Let's hope the other one is better."

"I've told you before, you can live with me as long as you need to."

Agreeing was easier than trying to convince her that I understood the complexity of her motives better than she did or at least would admit.

"Thank you, Mama, but it's time."

We left 4th and Gill and crossed the James White Parkway into South Knoxville. Knoxville had rightfully been dubbed the "Scruffy City" by an East Coast journalist years ago and the nickname had stuck. South Knoxville, separated from the rest of the town by three bridges, was on a whole other level. Where Knoxville was scruffy, South Knoxville was shabby and less polished than a chunk of broken asphalt.

There were also plenty of modest, well-kept homes, and even a few fancy ones on Island Home Boulevard next to the river, but the trashy median brought down the score of the whole area. Before Daddy died, we'd lived in two housing projects, five tiny apartments, and my grandmother's house. Four of those had been in South Knoxville. The community was as much a part of me as my eye color, unchangeable unless I wanted to poke them out to obscure my roots.

"Me and your daddy were living right up here on Baker when we brought you home from the hospital," Mom told me as we drove down Sevier Avenue. "I was so scared to give you your first bath, I called your mammaw."

The idea of my brash and intrepid mother calling her intimidating mother-in-law for help surprised me. "Why were you scared? You helped raise a bunch of your younger siblings."

"It's different when it's your own baby, Heather Pooh. No one gives you lessons. They let you leave the hospital with a little raisin-faced bundle and just expect you to keep it alive."

"Did Mammaw do a good job?" I asked.

"She had you bathed and snapped into clean clothes before I could sit down with a cup of coffee. She washed you under the kitchen faucet like a head of cabbage."

"I'm glad you didn't accidentally drop me."

"Oh, I did that plenty," Mom admitted. "You were the squirmiest baby. You turned out alright, though."

The Southwood apartments looked decent from the outside. The upper halves of the buildings were covered in an outdated rustic wood paneling, but the parking lot was free from litter and no one's stereo was turned loud.

We met the property manager in the office. She asked me where I worked, and I told her. Her face suddenly glowed as if she'd rubbed on an iridescent foundation. "I love Clinique!" she exclaimed. "Say, when's their next Bonus Time?"

As annoying as it was to have capitalistic ambassadorship thrust upon me, I had to admit that there was something nice about piggybacking on someone else's good reputation. I assumed this was how celebrities' and senators' children felt when the velvet rope was unclipped, and they strolled past the desperate throng through no merit of their own.

"Well, if I get this apartment, I'll be sure to remind you," I said jovially.

The three of us walked across the street and around the back of the largest building. The rear apartments were next to a clean-looking pool with its own parking. The complex appeared to meet the acceptable standard in Knoxville – decent, no frills, and no comprehension of the need for frills.

The property manager unlocked the door of an empty ground floor unit. Inside, the apartment was cool and quiet. Plain beige carpet, as opulent to my trailer-bred self as the most luxurious fur rug, provided a cozy insulation that made me want to curl up and take a nap. The kitchen was small but complete, big enough for a microwave and equipped with a full-size oven and refrigerator to store my TV dinners and fast-food leftovers.

"There's a *dishwasher*," I said ecstatically, running my hand along its black pebbled panel. Washing dishes by hand was nauseating. Our trailer had come equipped with a dishwasher, the first we'd ever had, and for two years, my hands did not once plunge into a soapy sink and feel a single water-logged Rice Krispie or greasy skillet.

Then, one dark morn, the dishwasher broke. Since we

were more broke than it was, it had remained empty and useless since then. Handwashing dishes, even when they were rinsed beforehand, reminded me of swimming in Tennessee's murky lakes. If something touched your hand under the water, you couldn't be sure if it was a stick, a catfish, or a water snake. I'd never been a fan of recreational terror.

"Ooh, fancy!" Mom replied.

The apartment bedroom and closet were twice as big as what I had in the trailer, and the bathroom grout was mostly white. There was no smell of mildew, cigarettes, or bug spray in the air. It was a blue-collar vision of loveliness.

"How much is this place, again?" I asked.

"If you sign a one-year lease, it's $330 a month," answered the property manager. I'd already crunched the numbers, but I did the math in my head once more. If I could keep my grocery budget low and reduce the infinite number of medical bills I was paying, I could scrape by, provided the transmission in my giant Oldsmobile hoopty didn't decide to ignite one morning on my way to work.

Like my decision to attend Cumberland, trying to parse whether to strike out on my own when I was barely treading water financially was impossible. Cumberland had been a smashing success – minus the student loans, of course – until it wasn't. Hard work and planning only seemed to take me so far. The supposed safety net at home was really just a cleverly disguised spider's web, a habitat where I might get trapped forever simply because the widow who'd spun it had understandable hunger pangs.

"I'll take it," I said.

Several years before at the Tennessee Valley Fair, I'd eaten two chocolate MoonPies right before boarding a ride much too rough for my delicate constitution. Halfway through, I'd barfed the South's most popular treat all over myself. Despite my distress, the operators had not stopped the ride, and I was forced to remain until the bitter end.

After the words left my mouth, I felt much the same way I did that day at the fair. Only time would tell if I was making the right decision, or if independence was simply a puke fest waiting to happen.

"Let's go sign the lease, then."

Back inside the management office, I filled out paperwork and wrote the appropriate checks. The apartment was now mine.

"Well, how do you feel?" asked Mom when we were back in the car.

"Good!" I said forcefully. "Terrified."

"That's how I feel every day, Punkinhead," Mom said. "You just have to have faith that the Lord will take care of you. He has so far."

"Yes, His holy covering is like a leaky radiation shield," I teased. "Not perfect, but better than nothing, I suppose. We haven't died yet. That's true."

Mom huffed in frustration. "Well, I was going to take you out to lunch to celebrate, but now I don't want to."

"You're one to talk. You've cussed God so many times, I've lost count." Her heartbroken 5:00 a.m. rants after Daddy died were the soundtrack of my middle school dreams.

She understood by the lilt in my voice that I wasn't picking on her, only reminding her that our faith was a messy and enormously complicated thing. It wasn't fair to expect me to abide by the rules and traditions she'd mostly shunned. The three of us had survived the grief in our own ways.

"Shit fire, Heather. If you want to hear complaining, read the Psalms sometimes. All I do is tell the Lord what's going on. Ain't my problem if He never talks back."

"Fair enough. Now, where to you want to eat?"

"We haven't been to Perkins for a while. I'm in the mood for one of their queesydeesies."

I tried to translate. "You mean … quesadillas?" I replied confusedly.

"Yes."

"Perkins it is. You're going to help me move, right? And will you go with me to buy the things I need?"

"Of course I will. I can bring you some dishrags and more empty buckets from the cafeteria, too."

"I know I don't have any furniture yet, but if the only chairs I have to offer my friends are giant green bean containers, I won't invite them over. Thank you, though."

"We can check out Smart Cents after lunch, if you want. They have a bunch of furniture." Smart Cents was our favorite thrift store. It didn't smell too bad, and their paperbacks only cost a quarter. "I want you to know I'm proud of you, Pooh. My first apartment was a tiny room in a boarding house. I was scared every night I'd have to move back home, and that place was like quicksand. Moving out takes guts."

She'd astounded me. Surely one day my daughters and granddaughters would feel only the firmest ground beneath their feet, unencumbered by the dysfunction that clung to us.

"What if I screw it all up?"

"Then I'll be here to help."

Later, at Perkins, we clinked together a mozzarella stick and a queesydeesy in a toast to the unknowable future, one that hopefully resembled an exciting thrill ride rather than a regret-filled path strewn with recycled MoonPies.

～

MY NEW WORK FRIENDS helped to furnish the apartment. Keke tucked a gift card in my purse one day during a shift. Victoria, nicknamed Vic, talked her mom into giving me their spare couch and a couple of table lamps. The couch was the nicest I'd had in any place I'd lived, covered in cream upholstery and dotted with green and blue buffalo check. The furniture's preppy and proper look contrasted greatly with the rest of my 'anything goes' design aesthetic, which had been painfully forged during my grungy teenage years. I aspired to one day have an expensive matching set of cabriole-legged furniture, yet for now, my best secondhand pieces competed with unframed posters from Spencer's Gifts and a Big Mouth Billy Bass in the bathroom.

Soon, I'd created a space fun enough in which to entertain friends and cool enough to host Sissy for a night or two when she came home from school on breaks. I missed her immediately each time she left, grateful for the new relationship we were forging as adults. Sending her back to college with a shopping bag full of department store makeup and skincare was the only thing that made me feel better anytime I watched her drive away. It helped balance the scale of the leanest Christmases and birthdays. Our childhood celebrations had rarely aligned with payday.

The first day of Bonus Time was a success. A few shoppers were already waiting outside the metal caging of the front entrance before we'd even opened. During our morning meeting, our department manager reviewed the goals for the day, reminding us to take advantage of the crowds to meet our credit card quota.

Shilling for Proffitt's credit cards was no doubt the worst part of my job. I met my goal each month – barely – but I was morally opposed to any high-interest credit card that could only be used for the emergencies of a new pair of cute shoes or the latest Lenox Nativity figurine, even if some patrons could afford it. Taking ten minutes to process a handwritten application for the store credit card while a lady on her lunch break was waving a fifty-dollar bill at you was foolish. Clinique consultants got paid a small percentage of each sale on top of our base pay, and the faster we sold during Bonus Time, the more we made.

Proffitt's profits would never be as important as mine.

The meeting adjourned. The security team unlocked the metal caging and pushed it into hidden doors in the sides of the entrance. The shoppers rolled through in a wave, the lankiest, most efficient memaws reaching us first.

"I'm here to get my gift," they'd begin, as if they were whispering a password to a closed door and needed special words to receive their sample exfoliation cream.

"What may I help you with?" I'd reply. Six out of ten requested their only Clinique purchase of the year, the product we were best known for and the product that most easily met the $19.50 requirement.

"I want my yellow lotion," said the memaws, the careerists, the minivan moms.

I'd scoop the box off the shelf with one hand and with the other unfurl a bag with a single shake. After the box was inside, I'd slide the bonus bag full of freebies beside it. Someone had taped the lotion's UPC to the register, cutting several seconds off the transaction time. The products were scanned, money or cards exchanged, and the customers wished well and quickly sent on their way. Each consultant had her own rhythm, and combined, we were as harmonized as a symphony.

We also had a stock room in which to flee if things got too overwhelming in the moment. Sure, the pre-sale packages waiting to be picked up were stored there, too, but the walls were thick enough to withstand the heartiest cursing in case one of the memaws turned feral and tried to blame us for the color of the free lipstick inside the bonus.

By lunchtime, I still had enough energy to fight the lines in the food court. Although the excitement of the morning had spun me frenetically, I hoped the extra charge would see me through the afternoon without a panic attack. I'd come to understand that fatigue or overwhelm empowered the nasty little suckers to wage a full-blown war on my body, even with medication. Trying to enjoy the pleasant buzz of hard work without triggering a hellish hour of hyperventilation was an ongoing challenge.

I found an empty table away from the crowd and sat. I

dug into my lemon chicken and soggy eggroll, which was delicious even after sitting under heat lamps for part of the day. The table faced the cookie stand, and I thought I might buy a cookie, too, irresistibly drawn as I was to the rich, sweet smell of chocolate wafting from the ovens.

I wasn't afraid of challenges, even though I dreaded them. Working at the mall and living on my own was going ok so far. I'd discovered that there was a large group of shoppers who liked me just fine. Some were fat; some were shy; and some might have simply appreciated my 'anything goes' attitude towards the boring and restrictive beauty standards that kept us lashed to the lie of perfection.

I'd never be a bulldog. I was fine lying on the porch with the rest of the easy-going hounds. As long as I could pay the rent and satisfy my credit card-hungry capitalistic overlords, maybe it was ok to have fun and relax a little. When the time was right to return to school, I'd know. Like a friend said, it wasn't brain surgery — it was just eyeshadow.

WRECKED

*E*aster Sunday was off to a cruddy start. Mom had browbeat me into attending service at the little Methodist church down the road from the trailer. I wanted to sleep in.

We'd joined the church right after Daddy died, but I hadn't set foot there for years. I dragged myself out of bed just to make her happy. The day was overcast and soggy. While I looked cute in my dress and patterned tights, it was too cold to go without a jacket, which further diminished my desire to be there.

I left my apartment and took the back way to Karns, preferring to drive the twisty but quiet McKamey Road instead of busy Western Avenue. I'd probably driven down McKamey and every other Knoxville road a hundred times by now, never growing bored with the random elements of charm sprinkled through the streets.

Several of my favorites were Knoxville landmarks, like

Kay's giant ice cream cones and the airplane-shaped gas station on the way to Clinton, but there were plenty of smaller things that were just as spectacular. Spring was a week old, and had temperatures been warmer, the beautiful hedge of pink blossoms that blanketed the highest slope of McKamey this time of year would've already started their stretch towards the sun.

This morning, the flowers remained underground to keep warm. I wrinkled my nose unhappily as I passed them, turning both the windshield wipers and heater up a notch. McKamey was a two-lane residential road lined with subdivisions, and the 35-mph speed limit was more than appropriate. There was no need to rush, especially with the rain.

A car traveling in the opposite direction suddenly appeared in the curved intersection ahead of me. He was speeding and driving over the yellow double line as if he owned the whole thing.

"You creep," I said angrily, slowing down and pulling towards the right so I wouldn't get hit. In an instant, my tires lost their grip on the road, and my car left the pavement. The puffy suburban grass was as slick as glass from the precipitation, and it propelled me towards a mature maple tree. Terrified, I put all my weight onto the brake pedal, rising off my seat in desperation to try to stop the car. The car did not slow. It coasted directly into the tree.

I braced for impact, closing my eyes. I heard the crunch of metal as the front of my car smashed into the solid hardwood. My chest lurched forward and was caught by the seat belt. As the belt tightened to keep me safe, the soft material of my dress caused it to slip off my breast, where it settled close to my collarbone. My knees rattled against the dashboard painfully, scraping the tender skin beneath my tights.

The car shuddered to a stop. After the click of the seized engine came the hissing roar of the radiator. My insides were bathed in shock.

I have to get out of the car in case it catches on fire, I thought sluggishly.

I pushed open the heavy driver's side door, thanking God that what the old car lacked in coolness it made up for in protection. I'd hit the tree head on, yet I was conscious, and nothing felt broken — at least, not yet. My purse had spilled onto the floorboard. I grabbed my wallet before stumbling outside into the rain.

The driver of the other car was long gone. The man who lived in the house closest to the tree was already running towards me.

"Ma'am, are you ok?" he asked, concerned.

"I think so," I answered. The skin on my chest burned from the friction of the seatbelt. I rubbed it briefly and it burned worse. I looked down at my legs. My tights were shredded from thigh to shoe, and small beads of blood had formed under the latticework still attached to my knees.

"I'm going to call an ambulance," he said, "and bring you an umbrella."

"May I use your phone after that? I need to call my mom."

"Sure."

He was back in a flash. He handed me his flip phone and popped open the umbrella.

"Thank you."

"Police are on their way."

I dialed Mom's number. My hands were slightly trembling from the shock, the cold, or both.

"Mama?" I said when she picked up. "I'm ok, but I was in a wreck. I need you to come get me."

A lot happened in the next ten minutes. The ambulance, a sheriff's deputy, and Mom arrived all at once. My car was a total loss; any repairs needed would run in the thousands and wouldn't be worth the effort, even if we could find the parts. Like everyone else with a beat-up car, I carried only liability insurance and nothing for collision.

The paramedic checked my eyes with a light and felt around my collarbone. "I don't think anything is broken," she told me. "Might be a good idea to go to the hospital anyway. Sometimes injuries aren't immediately apparent."

Mom, who'd parked in the man's driveway, tottered

over to me as quickly as she could. She was also dressed for church and wearing her nice shoes, which were hardly made for rescue.

"Oh my God!" Mom said, wrapping me in a hug. "Pooh, are you ok?"

"I think so."

Once she saw I was non-concussed and talking, her usual personality roared to life. "You know, Heather, if you didn't want to go to church, all you had to do was tell me."

"You're *hilarious*," I simpered.

"Do you need to go to the hospital?" asked Mom.

"It's not a bad idea. It's up to her," said the paramedic. "Her pupils are normal. She's going to be sore, though." I'd had my fill of emergency rooms in college, and the avalanche of bills from two years ago was still far from paid. Dividing a hundred bucks over a dozen different accounts every month was about as satisfying as watching a glacier melt. Plus, it was a holiday, which guaranteed that every hospital would be understaffed and likely filled with higher priority patients.

"I think I'll skip the hospital," I answered. "If I start feeling worse, I'll come in."

I signed a release form, and the paramedics left. By then, a tow truck had arrived. Mom and I watched from under the borrowed umbrella as the winch pulled the smashed car across the grass and onto the platform trunk first.

"How am I supposed to get to work now?" I lamented.

"Christ on His throne," Mama groused. "Why does this crap always happen to us?"

"There's no way I can afford this."

"Heather Pooh, you know I'll help if I can, but I'm not exactly rolling in it right now. I can't fork over a bunch of cash and pay in full like I did with this car."

Of course I knew that. "Can you take me to work tomorrow?"

"Yes, if you feel up to it. First, we need to get home and take care of those knees."

I'd have to feel up to it. I needed the money. I would also have to find a car, and quick. Mom and I lived thirty minutes from each other now, and there was no way we could carpool. I'd moved out of South Knoxville to share a place with a work friend so I could save on bills. It wasn't any closer to Mom's place than before. My apartment was near a bus line, but the city of Knoxville had a strange aversion to running buses after 6:00 p.m., and I often didn't leave work until nine.

Mom patched me up. We decided to head over to Mammaw's house for her traditional Easter dinner. Out of approximately thirty relatives, fewer than ten of us attended church on a regular basis, yet most of us subscribed to the tenets of Christianity – although asterisked. I had a lot to be thankful for, despite my horrible morning. I hoped to leave recharged enough to deal with the next looming financial storm.

We ate, then swung by my apartment for clothes, then stopped at a gas station to buy a Sunday paper. The Sunday edition of the *News Sentinel* was our favorite because it was the biggest and carried an entire section of classified ads.

Leaving the trailer together in the morning was easier than trying to coordinate pick-up times, and as much as I didn't want to admit it, I needed TLC. My brain processed trauma like a struck tuning fork. Just because I'd made it through the afternoon without upset didn't mean that I wouldn't wake myself up gasping from fear in the middle of the night.

I spread the classified section open on the couch and looked for deals. We'd had the same secondhand couch for years, and it was the same one on which I'd convalesced for six weeks during my days at Cumberland. It was saggy as ever. I could feel tendrils of unease wind their way into my mind. As had been the case my whole life, any forward momentum tended to shatter like glass if conditions were even slightly threatening.

"Mom," I began, "there's not a single inexpensive used car in this whole city."

"How much money do you have?"

"You mean, extra money? Like, maybe three hundred

bucks, *if* I skip paying the medical bills and only eat ramen this month." I threw the open paper over my head in defeat, covering my face like a tent. "Oh my *God*," I said angrily. "I want to find that man who caused the wreck and beat the crap out of him."

"You look like you already did," said Mom.

"What am I going to do?"

"Well, I guess tomorrow we'll go car shopping after I pick you up from work."

"Are dealerships accepting Monopoly money now instead of real cash?"

"If I have to help you finance a car, I will. I don't know what else to do."

Even though my mother was as maladapted by circumstances as a crooked shrub growing around a power line, she was always there when it counted.

"Are you sure you want to do that? You finally got your credit score back to normal." The cost of Daddy's funeral and a few low-balance credit cards had been enough to send her fleeing to Chapter 13 bankruptcy when I'd been in middle school. Cosigning wouldn't necessarily be ruinous. Things wouldn't go sideways unless I couldn't afford to make the car payments. How could I, really? My budget was already shaved leaner than a dried-out scrap of soap.

Preemptive shame and fearful acquiescence of

the possibility were apparent in my question, and she recognized it. "I don't see what other options we have," she went on. "We could get a loan and try to buy you another beater, which is fine until it needs expensive repairs. Or, I could ask one of your uncles to go with us to the dealership so they won't try to rip us off for being women, but none of them will buy you a car."

"Can't nobody fix this but your ole mama," she said with finality.

"I guess you don't want to try to sell the trailer and find some place to live together between Karns and East Towne, do you? My lease is up in a few months. I'd save more money that way."

"Lord, honey," she answered, "don't give up so easy. We've been on the ledge more times than we can count, and we haven't fallen off yet."

The lie was wild and beautiful, laughingly daring for a couple of patched-up pigeons with more than their fair share of scar tissue. I admired a faith so bold it was practically ludicrous. I wanted to believe her.

"Ok, Mama. If you say you can fix it, I'm going to let you fix it."

Later, as I lay scrunched on the couch with Cookie, who'd insisted on curling next to me, the rain began to fall again. The ambitious side of me, forever desperate to escape, was quiet tonight. I felt only safety inside our shabby trailer. The patter of raindrops against the aluminum roof was a lullaby, pushing me deeper into my dreams.

In no time, Mom was shaking me awake. "It's time to get up, Heather Pooh."

I sat up on the couch without opening my eyes. The movement stirred my body awake, and I groaned in pain. My shins, knees, and chest stung as if I'd spent all day in the sun.

"Ow," I said. "I hurt." Slowly, I put my legs on the floor, evicting Cookie in the process. I felt as stiff as an egg white beauty mask.

"Lordy mercy," Mom said. "Honey, look at your chest."

I walked over to one of the three diamond-shaped mirrors that lined the living room wall. A seatbelt-shaped purple bruise had bloomed across the area below my collarbone, reaching all the way past the edge of my armpit. I raised my right arm to test my range of motion.

I didn't get far. "Ow," I said again. "I don't think I could even hold a lipstick this morning."

"Woman, you better get on that phone and call in sick. You're too stove up to sell skin cream to a bunch of heifers today. I'm going to get you some ice."

I called my manager and explained what happened. She was insistent that I take the day off. "My manager said missing work was fine," I told Mom. "We can go look for a car, if we go slow."

Mom handed me a washcloth filled with ice. "First, put this on your chest for a while." The washcloth was rough and threadbare from being laundered over the years. I took comfort from it anyway.

"Alright, Lord," announced Mama. "We need to find Heather Pooh a car, and we don't need anything else to go wrong. Please don't give us some macho donkey as a salesman, or I might have to whoop him, in Jesus' name."

"Amen," I said.

～

THE PROCUREMENT OF MY new Kia Sephia went so smoothly, it was close to miraculous. By the end of the day, I was driving back to my apartment in a car as nice as Mom's. I wasn't exactly sure how it happened. While Mom's audacious petition of prayer temporarily boosted my belief in God (proving He didn't care how you talked to Him as long as you stayed in touch), I was uneasy about the looming payments. I'd convinced myself that I could afford the monthly $220 just long enough to add my signature to Mom's on the finance note.

The Sephia was only a year old. It came fully loaded and was the same muted red as an autumn apple. I felt like a fraud driving around town. I hadn't earned the right to a nice car.

I'd gone from living alone to needing a roommate. I was barely hanging on financially even before the wreck. Affording the car was technically possible, if I cut out lunch with the girls, karaoke nights, medical bills, and possibly, electricity. I didn't have the energy to bartend in the evenings or perform bad monologues on Market Square for extra money. I had to make things work as they were.

I survived the first payment. The month had been full of sack lunches and guilty glances at the unopened invoices of whatever radiologist or emergency room doctor I was stiffing. The second payment went ok, too, although I'd spent my medical bill money that month on food and a Tracy Turnblad costume for a party I'd thrown.

By month three, I'd received two collections notices about my medical debt. Some of the companies had never been happy with regular ten-dollar payments and demanded more, even as they cashed the checks I sent. Paying what I owed would've been infinitely more feasible if I only had one balance due each month, but none of the doctors I'd seen actually worked for the hospital. They were all independent contractors and billed separately. Multiply multiple doctors with multiple visits; add the asthma specialist and new medicines, and it equaled trouble. I could have made confetti with the number of envelopes I sent and received each billing cycle.

I was furious. How could anyone who wasn't born

rich get ahead? I'd taken advantage of every opportunity presented to me. I'd been derailed by poverty, depression, illness, and a dumbass driver. I had risen from the ashes each time, a trailer-park phoenix blazing from the glow of the cheap cigarettes her mother used to smoke, yet somehow lurching backwards with each rebirth.

Things had to change. I got a tip that MAC Cosmetics was hiring a new part-time makeup artist at West Town Mall. MAC was new to Knoxville and the most exciting thing to happen to makeup in years. MAC sold highly pigmented products in every color of the rainbow. They were inclusive, donated part of their lipstick sales to AIDS research, and designed each collection with an eye towards high fashion, like a bunch of avant-garde pirates building a sail with stolen couture scraps. Their employees were genuine artists as opposed to salespeople. Each had hefty sales goals, of course, but the products practically sold themselves. MAC was rumored to be the best-paying cosmetics counter around. Best of all, they were exempt from the soul-crushing store credit card requirements.

The MAC counter at West Town was sleek and modern. Hidden speakers pumped out club music every minute of the day, much to the annoyance of the surrounding cosmetics lines. The artists were dressed head to toe in black and wore no name tags. Their wardrobes and hairdos were flawless, their faces beat more fiercely than red carpet runways.

I really wanted the job. MAC's branding was multicultural and theatrical, reminding me that there was still a big world waiting to be explored outside Knoxville's orange-and-white city limits. Working there might be the closest I'd ever get to NYC or Paris, considering I could barely afford half an apartment's rent in the country's least polished burg as it was.

On the day of my interview, I brought along one of my most beautiful friends, Bess, to be my audition model. I was intimidated by the staff's perfect styling and the directions to "be creative" for the first makeup application. Being creative wasn't my industry strong suit. I had zero talent for drawing or painting. Even my stick figures turned out crooked. My strength lay in color theory and the simple, crisp utilization of flattering hues.

I tried to turn Bess into a bird, spackling her with bright jewel tones and extending eye makeup into her hairline. The look was supposed to evoke the haughty elegance of a peacock. Instead, the finished product called to mind a macaroni art project that had fallen off the refrigerator and gotten gnawed on by the family cat. Any technique passing muster with this avian nightmare was due only to Bess's glowing skin and big eyes and definitely not my talent. I did better with my second application, a typical special occasion look. The second attempt earned mild praise.

I was sure I'd blown it. In fact, I almost dropped the phone when MAC's counter manager called a few days later to offer me the job. The hourly pay was better – much better – than what I was currently earning. Unfortunately, the manager could only guarantee fifteen hours a week. If the business continued to grow, I'd be first in line for a full-time position. I was told it could take months.

Once again, I was left with an impossible decision. Until I was working full-time, I wouldn't be earning enough to pay for my extravagant lifestyle of a reliable car and the occasional dinner at Applebee's, not to mention the mountain of medical bills. However, I'd gone as far as I could with Clinique. Was it better to take a chance on a potentially much better job, even if I'd have to starve in the meantime?

The thought of never again having to utter, *"You know, you can save an additional 10% on your purchase today by opening a Proffitt's card,"* made me dance with joy. Never had a segue felt so clunky and predatory. Clinique encouraged their consultants to build rapport so our customers would fork over their phone numbers for future promotions. Any genuine connection we'd built during these interactions was severed the second we also started working them over on the department store's behalf.

Mom often quoted a Bible verse about how it was impossible to serve two masters. I thought I might write it on the bottom of my resignation letter if I decided to leave.

I considered things. I redid my budget. I prayed, then yelled, at God. (Sometimes it worked.) Finally, I broke down and called Mom.

"I don't know if I should take the MAC job," I said first thing. "I'll make a lot more hourly, but I don't have enough hours."

"Well, let's make a pros and cons list."

"Ok. Pros. They're super cool. They have affordable health insurance. Black clothing flatters me. And when they offer me full-time hours, it will be enough to live on, including the car and medical bills. Cons – it could take forever to be offered more hours, and even if they do, I might spend all my extra money on stupid things instead of sticking to my budget."

"Thank God you're still in forbearance with your student loans, child," Mom sighed.

"What's my problem, Mom? I do good for a while and pay my bills, and then some friends want to go shopping and I can't resist spending grocery money on a cute outfit. Why is it so hard to keep my nose to the grindstone?"

"If you had poor friends like I do, you wouldn't have this problem."

"Mom. You have to surround yourself with successful

people in order to be successful. Nobody in this trailer park is ever going to escape by draping themselves in sackcloth or an airbrushed t-shirt from the dollar store."

"Baby girl, it's hard because you ground your nose off years ago. We live so close to the bone there's no meat left. Give yourself some grace. Sometimes you need a little treat, so you won't go crazy. Why do you think I order so much from Avon?"

"Because diamonds cost too much?"

"Exactly," she replied. "Hang on a minute. Cookie's scratching at the door." I heard the phone graze against her hair and then her voice, faintly. "Dog, I just let you out five minutes ago. This is not a motel. You can't come and go as you please."

She turned her attention back to me. "Honey, I can't tell you what to do. If you want to work for MAC, go for it. God will work it out."

I hoped so. "Do you have any other advice? How can I stick to my budget better?"

"Why are you asking me? I already taught you everything I know. Just do the best you can and try not to get hit by a train."

"I love you, Mom."

"I love you and Cookie loves you, too. Bye."

The decision was mine alone. I remembered a few more

cons. I adored the entire East Towne Proffitt's cosmetics department, and I'd miss them terribly. The commute would be longer. I might lose my hearing from the MAC counter's obnoxiously loud music. MAC had potential, though, and if I could stay disciplined and steer clear of the railroad, I might come out on top.

～

ALTHOUGH MY SMOKY EYE never looked better, employment at MAC had not righted the ship. I alternated between paying medical bills and my car note for a few months so I could afford rent and food, which felt as helpful as labeling buckets to scoop water from a leaking boat. It made no difference whether I scooped from the bow or the stern. Either way, I was still sinking.

My lowest point came when I'd missed two car payments in a row. Mom was flat broke and so was I. I needed to catch up, not wanting a cigar-chomping repo baron to pay me a visit in the middle of the night and abduct the Sephia. Humiliated, I asked my friend Keke for a loan.

Keke had grown up in Nashville. She'd attended a well-known private girls' school growing up and was the daughter of a very prosperous pharmacist. She'd graduated from UT with a degree in social work while out-drinking and out-coquetting every hot, muscular showoff on Greek Row.

I was only halfway through my speech when she pulled out her checkbook.

"I got you," she'd said. "How much do you need?"

I named a figure, less than the amount I needed, but not so much that paying her back would be impossible. The last thing I wanted was to jeopardize a friendship over money.

"Thank you," I said gratefully. "Can I start repaying you next month?"

"It's not a loan. It's a gift. Just pay it forward one of these days and we're good."

Tears threatened because of her kindness, yet I didn't feel the hangdog shame so familiar to me in childhood. When non-profit do-gooders or rich churchgoers had knocked on our door in years past to offer impersonal Christmas gifts or a box full of dented (and sometimes expired) can goods, groveling was expected. We'd never risked souring their holiday spirit because we didn't want to be labeled as difficult or ungrateful. Upon further introspection, I realized that no rich churchgoer, as far as I knew, ever delivered charity to our house. Only the poor church mice who'd known similar struggle had dared set foot inside.

I'd learned to deaden the edges of feeling embarrassed around strangers. Asking friends for financial support was far more difficult, and it stung. I searched Keke's face to confirm her words.

"Are you sure?"

"I'm sure."

Keke didn't have an agenda. I didn't have to demean myself. She simply wanted to help. I could barely handle the relief of it.

Mom may have had a point about the impossibility of keeping up with the Joneses while living in a trailer park, but I wasn't wrong – rich and successful friends were worth keeping, especially when they were generous like Keke. A rich friend could hoist you out of a pit in a fraction of the time it took an organization to assign a volunteer, pack a food box, and deliver it to your drooping front porch with a condescending smile.

She tore out the check with a flourish and handed it to me. "Now that we have that settled, help me pick out which halter top to wear to Cotton Eyed Joe's tonight. We have some cute cowboys to wrangle. You date too many funky monkeys."

Since meeting Keke and the rest of my friends in cosmetics, I'd enjoyed a buffet of creative weirdos who either worked for Proffitt's or knew someone who did. I had casually dated a jazz trumpet enthusiast, an artist, and a martial arts teacher. I liked men whose taste ran to the unexpected, although there was no such thing as a wealthy creative in Knoxville. Perhaps I needed to follow my own advice and expand my horizons to include Keke's suggestions.

"I'll check out the cowboys. I'm not climbing up on any horses if I have my car, though. Thank you."

"The first time you see a cowboy wearing nothing but boots and a ten-gallon hat, you'll change your mind."

I considered what she'd said. In order to be successful, one had to surround oneself with successful people.

"Can I borrow a halter top?" I asked.

~

SEVERAL WEEKS LATER, I pulled the Sephia into Mom's driveway. I popped the trunk release, resting my head on the steering wheel in defeat.

After two colleges, two apartments, two employments, and two vehicles, I was back home for good. Like Icarus, I'd escaped to freedom but flown too close to the sun. Wings made of medical invoices and perforated car payment stubs were just as dissolvable as wax and feathers. I was free-range no more, a re-caged chicken shooed back into the rusty enclosure from which I'd flapped furiously away.

Worst of all, I was about to move into a smaller pen. Mom had managed to trade in the remains of our three-bedroom, two-bathroom trailer for a much newer two-bedroom, one-bathroom design. Her new trailer was fresh, pretty, and not nearly big enough for all my baggage, emotional or otherwise. The second bedroom was supposed to be Sissy's when she came home during the summer.

"Is that you, Punkinhead?" Mom called from the front porch.

"It's me," I said, "your oldest daughter. The one who's moving back in with her mother."

"And Cookie, too."

"Gawd," I muttered against my forearms.

Mom helped me unload boxes of belongings into the room Sissy and I were to share. "I'm glad Sissy lives in the dorms most of the time," I said. "She'd go crazy if she were here, and I wouldn't blame her."

"Heather, I told you before. You're welcome to stay as long as you need. We'll survive."

"I was so close this time."

"Shit happens, baby girl. The important thing is not to dwell on it."

It took three trips to completely empty my apartment. Once I'd turned in the keys, I drove back to Mom's new trailer. I felt oddly happy for a person whose fresh start was due entirely to failure. Mom and I had talked a lot about what would happen next. I'd finally be able to get a handle on my medical bills and still kick in some money towards the household expenses.

She'd also dangled an interesting proposition. Since I

wasn't yet working at MAC full time, had I thought about returning to school?

Cumberland College was in my rear view, sadly. Not only had my former suitemates graduated, but I'd finally admitted out loud what I'd known all along: earning a degree at a private school more expensive than the entire trailer park's mortgages combined was self-deception of the rankest kind. If I was determined to graduate, it would have to be from someplace cheaper.

Returning to school would reset my student loan forbearance, too. I was only a few semesters away from a diploma. I really wanted to hang that thing on my wall. A single piece of paper, as pricey as a fine work of art, might eventually be displayed in the trailer next to our Olan Mills family portraits and Sissy's Pantera posters, if things could stay righted for a while.

There was one thing left to do. It was going to hurt worse than a yellow jacket sting and yet, it had to be done. Soon after I'd moved back in with Mom, I returned the call I'd received.

"Hi. I'm calling about my car payment."

"Good afternoon," the agent replied. "Let me pull up your account." I heard the click of the keyboard and then a long pause.

"I'm sorry to inform you, but our bank has

started repossession action for the 2001 Kia Sephia. Multiple payments have been missed."

"Yeah, I know," I said grouchily. "What happens next?"

"The car will be collected in the next few days."

"When will that be? Do I have time to take it on a cross-country joyride before I'm back to hitchhiking?"

She didn't answer.

"I'm kidding."

"I understand," she said. "We have no further information at this time. My apologies."

"It's not your fault. Well, listen, I need to give you my updated address, so they'll know where to pick up the car."

"Please go ahead with your new address."

123 Loser Lane, Brokeville, Tennessee, I wanted to say.

"May I help you with anything else at this time?"

"I'm good, thanks. I mean, I'm not ... good. I just don't need any additional help at this time. Thank you. Have a great day."

I pressed the cordless phone's off button and disconnected the call.

"The end of an era," I told Cookie, who was sitting beside me on the couch. "You want some baloney?" I asked her.

Cookie's tail wagged in affirmation. I went to the fridge and peeled off two pieces of bologna from the pack. She waited impatiently for me to tear the meat into fourths. I grabbed a sleeve of saltines and plopped down in Mom's thrift store recliner. I assembled a cracker sandwich and watched Cookie eat her portion in one chomp.

"Here's to better days," I said. The dog replied with a burp.

~

"HEATHER," SAID MOM a few days later. "I think the repo man is here."

I looked out the front window. A gigantic tow truck was idling in the cul-de-sac, blocking Mom's driveway as well as our neighbor's.

"Yep," I answered. "Time to handle this."

I went outside and introduced myself to the burly fellow. He gave me a few minutes to remove my belongings before preparing the car to be towed.

"Thank you for making this so easy for me," he said. "You wouldn't believe the lengths people go to trying to hide their cars."

"Really?"

"Oh, sure. Sometimes they hide 'em at relatives' houses, or park 'em at the mall."

"I'd rather have this happen with as small of an audience as possible, personally."

"I hear that," he chuckled. "Well, have a nice day."

I went back inside to watch it happen.

The repo man took his time fiddling with the tow chains. I spoke up. "I'm sorry, Mama. I know this is going to hurt your credit since you co-signed."

"There was always going to be a risk, Heather Pooh. We'll be ok. Folks have been trying to count me out since the day I was born, and I ain't dead yet. Hard to get rid of a survivor."

"Is that what we are? Survivors?" I'd never felt particularly hardy. "I'm more like a clam. I like to stay safe and buried."

"That didn't work for Jesus, and it won't work for you," Mom said. "You were made to shine. You don't stop being sparkly just because you fell in a mud puddle."

Love for her filled my heart, covering the raw, stinging remnants of my pride like a cozy patchwork blanket. Neither one of us wanted me to be here, not really. Still, I was welcomed.

"We'll find another beat-up car we can pay cash for. In the meantime, you can borrow mine."

"Thank you. I can't say that enough."

"That's what mamas are for. You and Sissy are the best parts of your Daddy and me. Lord knows I want my girls to have better than we had."

Every inch of skin was sore from being kicked when I was down. I decided to stagger to my feet anyway. There was a lot riding on what happened next. I didn't want my parents' struggle to be for naught.

Eventually, something good will move us forward. Right, God?

If I found another crappy car, I'd be in the exact same situation I was after high school – as long as I didn't count the massive student loans, the panic attacks, and the feeling of regressing into my past faster than a samsara Ferris wheel falling off its axis. Maybe I was being given the chance to finish what I'd started at the University of Tennessee.

The repo man got the chains connected and activated the controls. The Sephia smoothly rolled up the heavy metal plates onto the truck's platform.

I'd survived a lot the last several years. I would no longer be intimidated by the size of campus or feel the need to conceal my fattest parts so as not to timidly intrude on those questioning my right to exist in a larger body. The desire to pursue acting was still there, although less than before. Working a full-time job proved that all the world *was* a stage, and eight hours of performance five days a week was more than enough attention from a fawning audience. I reserved the right to change my mind about it, though, if the right part came along.

In some ways, I was starting from scratch again, still nose-to-nose with poverty, still willing my arms to keep squeezing until I felt the crack of its windpipe before it fell to the floor, finally vanquished. There was freedom in the restriction of rock bottom. My only job was to keep climbing up. Nothing else mattered.

"I hope I'm making the right decision."

"You won't know for a long time," Mom answered quietly. "We never do."

The truck's diesel engine thundered up the hill past the trailer, causing the captured Sephia to bounce slightly with the effort. The tow truck took a right at the top of our street, and then it was out of my life forever.

I wished the future owner nothing but the best. I hoped the Sephia would bring them many years of happy driving.

"Thanks for bringing me here safely," I said in farewell.

"I'm going to put on my house shoes and watch *M*A*S*H* until it's time for bed," Mom said. "You want to join me?"

"I think I'll take a walk instead."

There was much to plan, and I needed to clear my head. I exited the trailer and walked up the edge of the hill, following the path of the tow truck. What was that stupid saying? Life was a journey, not a destination? Easy platitudes were worthless when the fastest mode of transportation I'd ever had was now speeding its way back to the dealership.

Even so, I owed it to Mama, Daddy, and Sissy to keep pushing forward. The crash cost me dearly, but the experience had moved me a little further down the road. Maybe the next rest stop would have an opulent hotel and fancy fast-food restaurants, so I could bask in luxury for a while before the next pile-up.

The beginning of fall semester was a week away, and I felt good. I'd followed Mom's advice and re-enrolled at the University of Tennessee. I'd just finished summer term, cramming a semester's worth of leftover science and humanities classes into eight weeks. Re-enrollment meant adding to my mountain of student loans, but the in-state commuter tuition was a fraction of the cost of Cumberland's, which idiotically made it a bargain.

Now only two semesters stood between me and a Bachelor of Arts degree. I thought about scrapping my long-established Theatre major for something, well, more attractive to the 99% of employers who didn't know their Ibsen from their Brecht. Unfortunately, a new major would have delayed graduation by eighteen months, and I was already four years behind. I hoped that a college degree, no matter the subject, was far more useful than not having one at all.

Now that I'd returned to campus and things were back in motion, I'd popped free from the unrelenting pressure of inertia. My finances were holding steady between what I earned from my job and the small excess provided by student loans. My grades were good, and I no longer dreaded the long commute from the trailer park since the end was in sight.

UT didn't scare me the way it had right after high school. In fact, I'd triumphantly marked the site of my former failure by asking my handsome science graduate instructor out on a date after the end of summer semester. He accepted, and while we ended up having less chemistry than a couple of noble gases, I thought it quite fitting to tinkle on the department fire hydrant where I'd flunked my first class.

Mom didn't want me to date again until after I graduated. She might as well have asked me to stop breathing. I longed for a loving relationship. Until he arrived, I was happy to speed things along by testing the waters with a variety of men. My social life had become a Whitman's Sampler filled with everything from acoustic emo dudes to tuner car aficionados, yet I was still left unsatisfied after a bite or two.

"Heather, if you're waiting for a man to make you feel whole, you're gonna be waiting a long time," Mom had said in exasperation after one of my dates. "Why not focus on yourself until graduation?"

"I don't want a man to make me *whole*," I answered, slightly offended. "I want a man to appreciate how special I am. There happen to be some cute guys that I don't mind spending time with until I find the right one."

"That guy you brought by the house a few weeks ago was *not* cute. He looked like a country bootlegger dressed like a gingerbread man. Smelled like one, too."

I huffed. "That wasn't gingerbread, it was patchouli. And he may look a little goofy, but he creates incredible mixed media canvases. He's also a pretty good kisser."

"If you need to kiss somebody, kiss the dog," said Mom, unimpressed.

"There's no use trying to explain this to you. You haven't wanted to date since Daddy died. Why is that?"

"I tried early on, if you'll recall, but you girls ran 'em all off."

"It's because they were losers."

"I believe you just proved my point, Heather Pooh."

Out of curiosity, I set up an online dating profile to widen the net. Knoxville yielded nothing of interest, so I set the parameters to include the whole state. That did the trick. Suddenly, my inbox was full of nibbles from places like Johnson City and Wartburg, towns even tinier than Knoxville where I might be worshipped like a queen.

Some of the messages were inarticulate; many were devoid of effort, lazy men casting *"hey"* or *"what's up cutie"* to my inbox the same way they fished – used to catching only the dumbest creatures with shiny artificial lures, and not even willing to get their hands dirty by using actual bait. I had no patience with these clowns.

One evening, I logged in to find an intriguing message from a man in Nashville. The email was clever, thorough, and respectfully flirty. He'd referenced *The Simpsons*, which was my favorite show, and made fun of his own accent, which wasn't American. His self-deprecation immediately put me at ease. The accent that poured forth from my mouth sounded like an untuned banjo and was just as loud. I knew what it was like to wish for a vocal coach.

I read every word of his profile. He was older than me and handsome in a craggy way. His hair was cut closely on the sides and shaped into a salt-and-pepper fauxhawk. If Iggy Pop had a brainy younger brother who was into wearing shirts, it might have been this guy.

Under *Profession* he'd typed *writer*. I held my breath to stop my heart's excited galloping. I had to know more. If he was a writer with a non-American accent, and he also happened to be kindhearted and eloquent, I'd have to take care not to keel over from the potential romance of it all.

I didn't want to pre-emptively swoon until I had more info. I replied to his message with a dozen questions, mostly about his career. The man responded an hour later with a thorough CV and more flirty banter. I was impressed. He was the author of three books. One of them won a prestigious award in his home country. Several national publications had published his freelance work, including a controversial series about the many shortcomings of American healthcare. By all accounts, he was successful.

If you care to know my thoughts on subjects ranging from politics to my cat's finicky appetite, I have a blog, too. Enjoyed your questions and looking forward to more. Sweet dreams, Simpsons fan.
Finn

I smiled slyly. Finn had to be a pseudonym. No one that interesting with that impressive of a résumé would also have a sexy name. I didn't mind. His real name could have been Norbert Grasseater or Donnie Earl Dookiebutt or a snoozer like John Smith. I liked my name. Not everybody was as lucky. If calling himself Finn put more power in his pen, I was happy for him.

I signed off for the night and made plans to swing by the library after class. I wanted to search our periodicals section to see if I could find Finn's articles and read his blog, too. I was the most excited I'd been about a guy in years.

I fell asleep and dreamt of him. In my dream, he sat in a barber chair in front of me while my pomaded hands smoothed the sides of his fauxhawk over and over. After a few passes, his hair lifted completely off like a Mr. Potato Head toy, and I apologized profusely for exposing his baldness. What that meant, I didn't know.

~

THE UNIVERSITY OF TENNESSEE had an impressive library, but Lawson McGhee, Knoxville's main public branch, was my favorite. The public library had been my second home since I was old enough to endure Mom wiping zwieback crumbs off my hands so I could touch the picture books. The library had taught me much about the world since then. It was also our family's go-to for free entertainment and frankly, survival. Lawson McGhee's climate-controlled stacks had saved us from two sweltering summers after the trailer's air conditioner stopped working.

The librarians who worked in Periodicals, which was tucked away on the third floor, could find anything. After one made a request for material, the librarian would disappear into what looked like a city block's worth of shelves and emerge a few minutes later clutching a box of microfiche or bound volumes, disheveled but victorious. If Finn had published anything in the last hundred years, I'd be reading it soon.

Once inside, I hurried to one of the online catalog

terminals. I typed in Finn's name on a whim, just to see what popped up. I gasped in elation. Lawson McGhee carried his most recent work of fiction, and it wasn't checked out.

I hurried over to the fiction shelves, where books were organized alphabetically. My eyes laser-focused on the spines. I saw his name immediately. I plucked his book from the middle of the row and looked at the cover. The artwork was noirish with a dark color palette. A drawing of bound woman wearing a negligée was prominent above the shadows. Her expression was mild and ignorant, meant to represent her victim status, I assumed. Her Victory rolls were pinned firmly to her head, even as her cartoonishly perky bosom threatened to fall right out of her see-through top.

My mind registered faint disgust. I read the description on the back cover and relaxed a little. Finn had written a story about a murder cover-up. It made sense that the artwork was distasteful. I was sure that publishers cared more about profits than they did about talent, otherwise they'd all be unemployed. Gore and sex sold, and this book seemed to have both. If they were looking for a way to get noticed, they'd found one.

I tucked the book under my arm in a way that concealed the drawing on the front and headed to the third floor. Like always, I hung back from the Periodicals entrance for a moment to catch my breath after climbing the stairs. I again studied the cover. Finn's picture was different than the one on his online profile, yet it was unmistakably him. A hot *ting* of adrenaline pricked the middle of my chest. I was having fun with this little investigation.

Within seconds, a librarian with perceptive eyes and a lumpy bun hoisted a volume of old magazines onto the table I'd occupied. She'd found Finn's article about the American healthcare system. I dug in. It was a good read. Having experienced years of inadequate care due to poverty, I agreed with nearly everything he'd written.

He grew up in a country with socialized medicine. He'd had access to basic care even though he'd grown up in housing projects, with no family to speak of except his father. My heart swelled with compassion and solidarity. We had something very important in common. Poverty was a leveler like no other; it didn't matter if only one of you liked folk music or you couldn't agree on what movie to watch. Once two people bonded over going to bed hungry, only gale-force winds could destroy their respect for the other's humanity.

I finished in Periodicals and returned to the first floor to check out Finn's book. I dove in as soon as I got home. I read it in a couple of hours, temporarily ignoring the paper I needed to write for Theatre History. The story was interesting and well-written, despite a depressing ending. I sent a quick message to Finn, informing him of my discovery.

The next morning, Mom was sitting in her recliner reading his book. As soon as I entered the room, she turned it face down on her lap to keep its place.

"Is this the same Finn that you're talking to online?" she asked. Her eyes were enlarged by the magnification in her glasses, adding an extra layer of scrutiny.

"Yeah," I said. "What do you think?"

"I don't like it."

"Why not?"

"It's too dark. If someone's not burying a body in a deep hole, they're passing out on a dirty motel bed because they've had too much gin."

I was irritated by her assessment, even though it was perfectly reasonable.

"It's dark because it's about a dark subject. You can't hack off someone's pinky and then expect them to go to a pie shop for afternoon tea."

I didn't know why I was defending him. I barely knew the guy.

"Well, excuse me, your majesty. I'm not being unreasonable. The Bible says that what comes out of the mouth starts in the heart. I *wish* he would write about tea and crumpets."

"Good Lord, Mom. It's too early for a sermon. I've not even had breakfast yet. May I remind you that Stephen King writes all kinds of crazy stuff and both of us love it? I don't hear you judging *his* work."

"Stephen King ain't the one trying to date my daughter. Look, just don't get yourself thrown into the back of a smelly Buick and tossed off a bridge, ok?"

"Fine." I poured a big slug of orange juice to keep my mouth occupied.

～

FINN SENT SEVERAL MORE emails before asking for my phone number one afternoon. I typed it into the message box with a squeal of excitement. I made sure to give him my cell number and not Mom's landline. The idea of Mom screening calls to protect my questionable virtue was so embarrassing, I wanted to slump to the floor in a faint.

My phone immediately began to ring.

"Is this Finn?" I answered flirtatiously.

"Is this the famous Heather, then?" he replied. I laughed throatily, thankful I'd inherited the timbre of my father's rich radio voice. Finn's accent wasn't posh, but it was so completely different from my own, my heart skipped a beat. He sounded like misty mountain morns and vacations where groups toured old castle ruins.

"Yes, but no autographs, please."

It was his turn to laugh. We began to talk at the same time, tripping over each other because we had much to say. We chatted until it was time for me to go to work.

"How long have you lived in Nashville?" I asked towards the end of our call.

"A year, and I hate it. Tennessee is the most backwards state in this country. My roommate and I moved here from Chicago. The difference is stark. Anytime I have a chance to leave the city, I do."

I bristled. Tennessee was full of idiots, and perhaps we had more per capita than Illinois. We also had hundreds of thousands of decent people who would literally share their last bites of food with stray animals and give strangers the Nascar-branded shirts off their backs.

My silence was stony. "Obviously, you're a clear exception," Finn added quickly.

"I hope one day you'll get a chance to meet the rest of the good people who live here. There are quite a few of us."

"*Blast*," he said lightheartedly. "I'm terribly sorry. Half the people I meet in Nashville say something stupidly racist in the first thirty seconds and it's unbearable. I don't mean to write off the whole state. Forgive me?"

I knew exactly who he was talking about. "Of course

I forgive you," I said. "We have a bunch of those fools in Knoxville, too. They think they have carte blanche to share their horrible opinions with anyone who's white. I get it."

"Was that a pun?" he asked. "I do enjoy traveling to Atlanta. I book a lot of events there. Never been to Knoxville. What's it like?"

I thought about it. "Like sticking your hand in muddy water. Depends on where you are in the lake. Could be a gentle current, could be a water moccasin you just woke up from a nap. That's what makes it interesting." Full of idiots or not, I wasn't about to compress my hometown into a few reductive sentences to satisfy the curiosity of an unfamiliar. Finn could discover the nuances of the Scruffy City on his own.

"Dolly Parton's from around there, isn't she?"

I felt my body shift into attack mode. Tennesseans were as dangerous as napalm to anyone who insulted our patron saint.

"Yes, she's from Sevierville, originally. That's about thirty minutes down the road from here, if you drive fast."

He'd need to choose his next words wisely.

"What a talent she is," Finn replied. "One of the best songwriters of all time."

I exhaled with deep relief. "Damn straight," I answered.

"Would you be averse to having dinner with me if I were to visit Knoxville?"

I was hoping he'd ask something like that.

"I would very much enjoy having dinner with you. I assume you like biscuits, gravy, and fatback?"

He laughed. "Those are vegetarian, right?"

"We'll ask the chef to omit the possum meat."

He again laughed, and I took stock of my thoughts while he did. *Girl, you are about to embark on an exotic expedition to an ancient site. You better make sure to get your shots before you start traveling internationally.*

I'd trekked as close to his border as I wanted to for now. "Well, I've got to leave for work. I really enjoyed talking to you."

"Same," Finn said. "Talk again soon?"

"You bet. Bye."

There were no passports for affairs of the heart, or vaccinations, for that matter. If I were to launch this ship, I'd have to do it like the explorers of old – boldly, blindly, and full of outrageous ego.

~

LIFE HAD GOTTEN PLEASANTLY busy. Between work and school, I found time to shoehorn in a stage-managing role as a favor to my favorite communications professor. Finding another mentor late in my college career was an unexpected blessing, and one I didn't take for granted. I'd aced Dr. Armbrust's Rhetoric class over the summer, and we'd hit it off immediately. He and his wife, Cecilia, a retired public school teacher, were old enough to forgo work and spend their time on back-to-back vacations, but they loved being a part of the educational field and refused to give it up.

Dr. Armbrust and another well-respected UT faculty member decided to stage a production of *God's Trombones*, a series of tableaux and songs based on James Weldon Johnson's book of poems adapted from Black pastors' sermons. The staging was simple, yet the idea was ambitious: start with presentations in a few local churches in hopes it would grow from there as word spread about the talented all-Black cast and spiritually gripping message.

Dr. Armbrust understood my new ambivalence about acting. With less than two semesters until graduation, I feared it was too late to leave my mark on UT's Clarence Brown Theatre. Coming to terms with this reality sadly did nothing to snuff out my love for performance.

"Why don't you come be our stage manager?" he'd asked. "We're planning on more shows in the future, and our troupe isn't tied to UT. Who knows, maybe there's another acting role for you down the road."

He said it lightly and sweetly, like he would to a child who was past naptime but hadn't started crying yet. I felt a tug of affection for both him and Cecilia, happy to be in their non-judgmental Methodist orbit.

"Please?" he added. "I'll dance at your wedding."

"You might be waiting a long time to mambo, Dr. A.," I replied. "I'll do it, though."

We'd started rehearsal immediately, and before I knew it, we'd been booked into a dozen churches. Stage managing only paid thirty bucks a show, but it was the first time I'd ever been paid for anything theatre-related, and I was terribly proud. The cast was friendly and exceptionally talented, and we got to know each other as the weeks passed. I often considered what Dr. Armbrust had said when he first offered me the stage manager job. Maybe there would be room for acting after graduation.

Finn and I continued to communicate regularly. Emails were easier, as we were rarely available when the other called. I found his two other books in online secondhand shops and ordered them. The novel that had won the distinguished award in his home country was a more satisfying read than the library find; it was a sadly touching story about the tumultuous relationship between a father and son. I also caught up on his blog.

The next time we talked I brought up the award. "What's it like to be celebrated like that? Do they throw you a party or what?"

"Nothing that exciting, I'm afraid. They mailed me a nice

certificate, and my agent took me out for drinks. I must say, it helps with book sales, as embarrassing as it is to admit."

"If I wrote a book and won an award like that, I'd probably fly a banner across Neyland Stadium during halftime. And if I didn't do it, my mom would. You must be very proud."

"Ah ... sure. It was almost a decade ago," Finn said. I could tell he didn't want to talk about it anymore.

Since we were about to change subjects, I decided to mention something on his blog that had pricked my curiosity, and not in a good way.

"So, I've been meaning to ask you," I began. "You mention a woman named Susannah on your blog sometimes. Who is she? Your roommate? Your ex? What?"

"Susannah's my roommate. We've known each other for years. She's more like a sister than anything else. I changed her tire in the gravel parking lot of a pop-up carnival one day. That's how we met."

"You mean the guy who hammers nails into his nose wouldn't help?"

"Susannah asked. He was on his lunch break and couldn't be bothered."

"Chicago sounds ... interesting," I said. "Did you guys ever date?" Knowing my own history with Davy, I had to ask.

"You can relax," Finn replied. "Susannah's gay."

"Relaxing now," I said with a laugh. "I'm happy to hear that, not gonna lie."

"Do you have plans this Sunday evening?"

"Why, Finn!" I feigned surprise. "Are you officially asking me out on a date?"

"I finally have some time to pop over to Knoxville. I'd love to take you to dinner."

"Sunday's busy for me. We have two performances that day." I calculated the hours I'd need to get home, shower, slip into a dress, spritz, tousle, and beat out my face so gorgeously he'd drop to his knees in devotion. "But I could squeeze in some time around eight," I said casually.

"Terrific," he answered. "Does Knoxville have any vegetarian restaurants?"

"Sure. Sunspot, on campus." Sunspot was popular and always busy. However, they were about as upscale as the grungy summertime entrepreneurs of my childhood who'd sold unregulated snowcones out of the backs of their rusty pickups. I'd be completely out of place in a restaurant full of sage-scented, vaguely blue customers who'd overdosed on colloidal silver. I knew almost nothing about vegetarian cooking. I grew up thinking the word for soybean meat substitute was *toefood*.

Too bad. I was going to look hot no matter what, even if the militant vegans and the wan nut-milk drinkers banded together and forced me to eat dessert sweetened with chopped dates and thoughts of world peace instead of the good kind of sugar.

"Shall I meet you there, or would you like me to stop by and pick you up?"

I thought of Mom answering the door with a twelve-gauge shotgun perched on her hip the same way she'd tote around a sticky-torsoed baby.

"*No!*" I said quickly. "Thank you. I'll meet you there." Regardless of my living situation, it wasn't the smartest idea to climb into a stranger's car, even if he *had* been a Selection of the Month.

"Until Sunday evening, my Southern siren."

The way his accent bent the *s* sounds made me blush hotly. I tried to play it cool.

"Southern? Yes. Siren? Only if someone steals my cornbread."

"Adorable thing."

I blushed again. "I'll see you Sunday," I said, and disconnected the call.

~

I TOLD DR. ARMBRUST and Cecilia about Finn. I hurried through my duties after the second performance, anxious to get home.

"Where is he taking you to dinner?" asked Cecilia.

"Sunspot. He's a vegetarian, and it's the fanciest vegetarian restaurant we have in Knoxville. I guess it's fine for a first date."

"Heather, Ralph and I want you to know that if anything goes wrong, or if you ever need a ride in the middle of the night, you call us. I mean it."

I was deeply touched. "Are you worried about this guy?"

"Not exactly. You have good sense, but even people with good sense sometimes find themselves in sticky situations. Ralph and I have extracted a few students from jams over the years. All I'm doing is passing along that same offer to you."

"Does that include bail money?" I joked.

"It has before," Cecilia said. "Try to stay out of trouble, ok?"

I hugged her before peeling out of the parking lot. Once home, I dressed carefully. I was pleased with the result. If my calculations were wrong and Finn wasn't impressed, I'd have to retire from dating altogether and start a detective agency or something with my equally single mother.

As I was leaving, Mom sized me up from the recliner. She said nothing.

"I already know what you're going to say," I said with an eyeroll. "Just don't come home pregnant."

"My work here is done," Mom answered, turning her attention back to *Reader's Digest*.

I shut the trailer door with a huff and drove my new old car to Sunspot. Street parking around campus was practically non-existent, so I pulled into a paved lot close to Fort Sanders Hospital. I needed the five-minute walk to the restaurant to stop hyperventilating and calm my shaky limbs.

I'd barely finished checking my reflection in the driver's side window when I noticed a man walking towards me from the top of the sloped lot. It was Finn.

My knees trembled under my striped dress. I waved to him. He paused, waved back, then crammed his hands into the pockets of his black jeans. Ugh. I hated black jeans. Still, the thrill of adventure made my heart pound faster.

He walked up to me, taller than expected. His height wasn't overwhelming, although he was the right size to change lightbulbs and swat cobwebs without trouble. His face was more lined than in his pictures, and his clothes hung big on his lean frame. The most obvious thing about him, besides his gelled fauxhawk, was the aura of softness he radiated. He wasn't soft like the warm embrace of a grandmother or a delicate cashmere turtleneck or even a roll of deluxe toilet paper. Instead, his softness was a squishy thing, greasy like a scoundrel who betrays the rules of a gentleman's duel and wins by shooting his opponent in the back.

Oddly, triumph filled my veins. There was nothing intimidating about a man who looked dishonorable. The only men who made me nervous were the genuinely good-hearted or the ones pretty enough to pass for cherubs. The specimen standing before me looked as insecure and petty as I, although prone to the same occasional bursts of genius. The only difference was that my talents hadn't yet been professionally lauded.

Finn's demeanor was stoic. He shifted his weight slightly from foot to foot, and I realized he was as skittish as an alley cat. I found that amusing, wondering if he'd decided whether my youth was arousing — or arresting.

One of us had to say something, so I opened my mouth. I was quite shocked to hear what tumbled out.

"Are you going to kiss me or what?"

Surprise lifted his eyebrows, transforming his forehead from smooth to Shar Pei.

I had just jumped out of an airplane and landed in the jungle with nothing to guide me but my own audacity. When I was this far outside of my experiential comfort zone, I apparently threw as much caution to the wind as a sightseer with a hallucinatory illness.

Finn did as I asked.

The smooch was nice, although I discovered a few

imperfections as we strolled hand-in-hand to the restaurant. I had a prettier mouth, for instance, and although I felt butterflies during the process, they seem to churn my stomach in turbulence rather than romance.

After dinner, we walked down Cumberland Avenue and up to World's Fair Park so I could show off a bit of my city. Our conversation flowed in person as it had over the phone. Luckily, Finn didn't say a single bad thing about Knoxville. Starting our date the way we did unexpectedly calmed my nerves, like getting bloodwork out of the way first thing at a doctor's appointment. I wanted to see him again.

We said goodbye around 2:00 a.m. "Perhaps you'll come visit me in Nashville next time," Finn said, embracing me.

"Maybe. That's a long drive. I'm not sure my car would survive a six-hour round trip."

"Susannah and I do have a couch you could sleep on, if spending the night would help."

A strong tingle cascaded over every inch of my skin. I could only imagine what my mother would say if she'd heard his invitation.

"We'll see how it goes," I demurred. We shared another kiss before getting into our cars, and then I was driving home as if it were a regular Sunday night. When I got back, I opened the front door of the trailer quietly. Mom was asleep in her recliner. She'd waited up for me. I covered her with a crocheted blanket and went to the bathroom to wash my face.

~

THE START OF SPRING semester came and went. I thanked God profusely when I hit the four-week mark, since I'd only survived three weeks of winter the last time at UT before I'd stopped going to class. *God's Trombones* had been extended month after month, with new churches added constantly. I still enjoyed being stage manager. Best of all, my grades were good, and I was expected to graduate in the summer.

Finn and I had fallen in love. Our schedules remained busy, and we only saw each other sporadically. However, after our first meeting in Knoxville, I became the recipient of a flood of floridly passionate emails that finally convinced me of Finn's gift for writing. I'd print them out and stuff them into my backpack to read during class, toggling between taking notes and swooning.

Even his short messages were effective, rendering me mushy-headed and desperate to see him.

Just a few words, my darling, before I head to Atlanta this morning. When will you stop tormenting me? I dream of you often but awake only to my loneliness. I love you.

He'd been to see me a few times but still hadn't met Mom, at my request. I was wildly protective of our budding relationship, and Mom was wildly protective of me. Like many mothers and daughters, strong love existed simultaneously with co-dependence. The second Daddy died, Mama became my responsibility. Fair or not, our perimeters of freedom were only as expansive as my ability to afford my own life, or her need for companions not put off by her brash demeanor.

Mom's protection was generally helpful, if somewhat maddening. She'd offered no more than a grudging acceptance of Finn. I couldn't shake the feeling that she was seeing something I wasn't. Then again, Mom had a deep fear of abandonment, most recently proven to be true after my father's death, and she'd always kept me clutched closer than a balled-up tissue in a mourner's fist.

"Mom's driving me crazy," I told Finn the next time we talked. "She doesn't like you. She's already made up her mind because you haven't been by yet to kiss the ring."

"That's too bad. I don't need your mother's approval. Neither do you."

"Boy howdy. You are definitely not from the South," I said dryly.

"Maybe I'm not the best to give advice, then. I barely knew my mother," Finn replied. "She left when I was young."

"I'm sorry, love."

"Nothing to be done about it now. Does your mother know I'm coming to your graduation?"

I stamped my feet with happiness. "Yes, and I'm so excited! You'll get to meet my sister and a bunch of relatives on my father's side."

"What are they like?"

"Sissy's awesome and so is the rest of my family. I would like to inform you, however, that most of them are hotheaded and the majority carry pistols. So, interact at your own risk."

"The women carry pistols, as well?" he asked, puzzled. How a crime writer managed to skirt awareness of this subject was truly baffling.

"Why do you think we have such big purses?"

"I can't say I'm looking forward to that, but I can't say I'm not, either," Finn said. "Will I need to pack heat at the next barbecue?"

"Yes, *if* you're invited."

"My charming Heather, when are you coming to Nashville to stay with me?"

"I've been thinking about it. When are you free?"

"Anytime this week. What do you say? Break free for a couple of days. You can borrow a pair of Susannah's cowboy boots. I'll escort you to all the awful tourist traps along Music Row, and we'll drink beer out of red plastic cups."

"Well, I guess I could skip school on Friday, spend the night, and leave Saturday evening. We have a performance Sunday morning."

"Wonderful. I'll start brushing the cat hair off the furniture now. Things should be tidy by then."

I chuckled. "I should go. I need to rearrange my schedule and switch some hours for work. Love you."

"Same, darling."

Friday morning was bright and sunny. I had the trailer to myself. I turned my stereo loud as I dressed and packed an overnight bag. Mom had already gone to work. She'd asked me to call her when I got to Nashville, and I promised I would. Before leaving, Mom paused at the door, clearly wanting to say more. In the end, she'd merely pressed her lips together and went on her way.

I made it to Nashville in time for lunch. I followed Finn's directions and found the parking garage for his building. Inside, there were plenty of exposed brick walls and funky industrial accents, obviously a recently renovated factory or similar. I didn't understand the appeal of paying top dollar to live in a walk-up that was reminiscent of a noisy workplace. I felt the same way about camping or anything else that shared elements with poverty. I would never sleep on the ground outside or wake up with asbestos-laden whitewash on my clothes unless forced to.

I waited at the end of the hallway for almost a minute, trying to compose myself. Visiting a boyfriend's house for the first time was like visiting a museum. How he folded his bath towels was just as illuminating as learning about King Tut's military strategy or the type of paint da Vinci used.

I knocked on the door. Finn opened it, clad in a gray t-shirt and chinos. His feet were bare.

"You're here," he said. I was barely inside when he swept me into his arms and kissed me until I bowed backwards. I felt like the cat trapped underneath Pepé Le Pew.

I pulled away from him, embarrassed. Making out in front of others was grosser than people who ate pimento cheese with their mouths open.

"Hey, why don't we wait until we have a little more privacy? Let's not put on a show in your living room," I suggested.

"About that," Finn said. "I wanted to surprise you. Susannah's not here."

"What do you mean?"

"She's on a business trip this week. We have the condo to ourselves."

His announcement didn't make me uncomfortable. A world of possibilities had suddenly opened in front of me. I was only prepared for some of them. Mom's edict on intimacy had been nailed to my brain since high school. I wasn't worried about the physical ramifications of any decisions I made — pistols weren't the only protection a smart women might tuck into her overnight bag – yet I wasn't sure if I was ready for a full twenty-four hours of practical communion without the buffer of another human nearby. We hadn't advanced to the nose-picking or open-door-peeing stage of our relationship. I kind of hoped we never would.

Sensing my hesitation, Finn added, "You can still sleep on the couch, of course. And you should certainly leave if I've made things awkward." His mouth twitched flirtatiously with faux repentance. "I hope you'll stay, though, or I'll be forced to write bad poetry as I sit alone with only the cat to keep me company."

My boyfriend and my mother shared a common goal. Both seemed intent on holding my pride hostage. I had no intention of slinking home early, only to be silently audited by Mom as we sat watching television. I'd be the loser no matter who won.

Fearing the unknown but barreling towards it just the same, I reached up to give Finn a peck on the end of his nose.

"*Rascal,*" I said, wrapping my arms around him and kicking the door shut behind me.

～

I EMERGED FROM THE condo Saturday evening, ready to drive back to Knoxville. So far, the only peculiar trait I'd uncovered was Finn's refusal to move his cat, Krupa, off the kitchen counters during meals. I thought people who let their cats' litter-ridden paws and uncovered exit systems occupy the same space as their cutting boards were in dire need of therapy. However, I could only fight a war on so many fronts.

"I'll call soon," Finn said.

I tousled his hair, dirty with day-old mousse. "Ok," I replied.

He gently grabbed my forearms and drew me close.

"You know I'm going to marry you," he told me.

I knew. "Those are bold words to be throwing around right as I'm leaving."

"So, stay," he said, trying to maneuver me back inside.

"You're incorrigible," I told him. "I've got to go. Time to shift my focus to less earthly things. Tomorrow's performance is at a Presbyterian church."

"I find your dash of religion quite amusing. At least you're only sprinkled and not soaking in it like most of the people around here."

"I contain multitudes, my love, like a gourmet bouillabaisse."

"More like the pepper flakes in that disgusting white gravy you eat." He kissed me goodbye. "Drive safely."

When I got back to the trailer, Mom was sitting in her recliner sharing scrambled eggs with Cookie.

"Did you have fun?" she asked, munching on some toast.

"It's bedtime. Why are you eating breakfast?"

"Just making sure I had the energy to get through the night if you got home late."

"Mom," I began, "I'm ok. Really. You might as well get used to Finn. He mentioned marriage earlier today."

Her mouth was full of eggs, but her eyes bulged in a way that left no doubt as to what she was thinking.

"Listen, I've got a busy day tomorrow. I need to go to sleep. Thanks for waiting up for me." I patted the top of her foot to say good night.

She chewed her bite quickly and threw her toast crust to the floor. Cookie gobbled it up.

"Good night, Punkinhead. We ain't through talking about this."

I'd be hearing Mom's opinions on her deathbed, or mine, whichever came first.

She'd calmed down by Sunday evening. I explained things more thoroughly, omitting any details sure to raise her blood pressure. A lot was riding on Finn's performance at my graduation. He didn't care about impressing Mom or any of the rest of my family. I wasn't sure if that was a byproduct of his age, his scant upbringing, or something else. I gave him the benefit of the doubt because Mom wouldn't, and I hoped everyone would relax once they got to know him.

I considered my options after graduation. My boss at MAC had been recently promoted to a store in Atlanta, and

Finn was in Atlanta as much as Nashville. Knoxville was safe as milk, but unpolished and changeless. I'd finally healed enough to lurch forward into a new chapter, even dunked in trauma and breaded with scar tissue as I'd been.

I mentioned it to Finn the next time he called. "I've been toying with the idea of moving to Atlanta. What do you think?"

"Why Atlanta?" he asked.

"Bunch of reasons. First, I could see you more often. You're in Atlanta almost as much as Nashville. Didn't you tell me you've thought about moving there?"

"I've thought about it, yes."

"Atlanta also has about a billion cosmetics jobs and I'm sure they pay better than Knoxville. My boss from MAC already works in Atlanta, and she likes me. I could try to get a job at her counter. If she's not hiring, I have enough experience to get a gig anywhere. And I'm ready for a change. I've never lived in a big city before. I want to give it a shot. Atlanta must be more interesting than what I'm used to."

"That sounds reasonable, darling, but if you move, move for yourself, not me. I can just as easily meet you in Knoxville."

A tine of anger pricked me. It was a small thing, really, yet my skin reacted as if I'd been poked for real. Didn't he know by now what we were committing to if we stayed in Tennessee?

"As long as I'm living in Knoxville, my mom and I are a package deal," I said as evenly as possible. "It's … complicated. If you and I end up together in a different state, it makes everyone's lives easier. Believe me." Finn was well aware of my frustrations with Mom and the general difficulty of hurtling oneself out of poverty. I needed to draw the map for us, which only had one route — escape.

"I believe you, but if things didn't work out between us, I wouldn't want you to have uprooted your life."

The tine of anger that poked me before turned into a forkful, possibly even the big one brought out at Thanksgiving to help serve the turkey.

"Were you or were you not breathlessly mentioning marriage to me as recently as last week? Why should some … inevitable decay of our relationship be top of mind?" I fumed.

"It shouldn't, my beauty. Of course I want to be with you. I've simply had much more experience with this than anyone should. I've been around since the Stone Age, remember?"

I could almost see Finn's crooked smile through the phone. It was one of my favorite things about him. I let my anger dissolve.

"The Pleistocene Age, really." I teased. "I understand, and I appreciate your caution. I think it's time for a new adventure, though. I really do."

"What about your acting troupe?"

"That's a tough decision. If I found a good group in Knoxville, though, I'll probably find ten in Atlanta. Literally five million people live there."

Jumping ship in Knoxville *was* a risk, especially if I ended up drowning in Atlanta anyway. I would never admit it. The prospect of a wildly passionate love affair, even a slightly bewildering one that had the potential to blow sky-high, was preferable to just about anything life had to offer, except a lottery win.

Anyone who thought differently could mind their own business. Some would call me crazy for trading a trailer full of unhealthy interconnectedness for a relationship that might turn out to be even worse, but I preferred the term 'romantic.'

"What will you do next?"

"Besides study for finals?" I groaned. "Send out some résumés, I guess. Research where I want to live."

"I'm very excited for you, and for us."

"I love you, Finn."

"I love you. Study hard. I'll see you at graduation."

To my great surprise, Mom was supportive of my move to Atlanta.

"So, he'd still be in Nashville, and you'd be in Atlanta, in your own apartment?"

"His name is Finn, Mom. Yes. I'd have my own

place. Eventually, if things worked out between us, we'd get married."

"As long as you're not shacking up, I support you."

"For Pete's sake," I scoffed. "Why does it matter if we have a marriage license or not? Plenty of people live together in monogamous relationships without having to pick out a china pattern or starving themselves to get into an expensive dress."

"Child, this is not about a wedding. It's not about Jesus or what some sanctimonious butthead thinks about folks' bedrooms, either. Marriage protects you legally. If you live together and he dies first, you won't get any survivor's benefits. And if you split up after twenty years, you don't get a damn thing from that house you didn't pay for yourself, even if you kept every inch of it clean and washed his dirty drawers, too."

"Ok, ok. You've made your point. Anyway, I *want* to get married."

"Things are finally going good, Heather Pooh. If you want to try something new, I say go for it."

"Thank you, Mama. I know you're going to like Finn once you get to know him. Promise you'll give him a shot."

"I will," she relented.

"I guess it's settled, then. I'll start looking for jobs after I'm finished studying."

I skipped down the hallway happily, like a little kid. A bright path had opened in front of me, and I was ready to follow it.

The last few weeks of spring semester flew by. I was deep in study for finals and busy with graduation preparation and plans for the move. Since many in the *God's Trombones* cast were also students, Dr. Armbrust announced a summer hiatus for the show. I told him and Cecilia of my plans and thanked them for the opportunity, grateful the break would allow time to find another stage manager.

"If Atlanta doesn't work out, you've always got a place with us in Knoxville," said Dr. A.

"But don't you dare give up your dreams just to marry Finn," added Cecilia. "He's the lucky one, not the other way around."

I briefly considered how different my life trajectory would have been if I were their daughter. No early death of a parent, no poverty, only intelligent and loving discourse in a socially conscious household, happily earning degree after degree until there wasn't enough room left on my office door for all the honorific titles.

I heard Mom's voice in my head. *Shit happens, baby girl.* What a pointless endeavor, playing what if. At least I'd been blessed enough to meet them in the first place. I could count on one hand the number of people who'd come running if

I needed help in the middle of the night. Dr. Armbrust and Cecilia were two of them.

"I love you both," I said, hugging them in turn. "Thank you for believing in me. And Dr. A., I fully expect you to dance at my wedding, like you promised."

They shared a look I didn't understand. "We love you, too," said Cecilia. "We'll be there, no matter where you get married."

Before I knew it, I'd finished taking my first final and was on my way home to share good news with Mom. I'd received a voicemail from a cosmetics manager at Perimeter Mall in Atlanta who wanted me to drive down for an interview. This brought the total to three so far. Even though my former boss at MAC wasn't hiring, she'd been delighted to hear from me and told me to check back.

My plan was to take a day trip to Atlanta after finals and come back with a job. Once I knew where I'd be working, I could start apartment hunting. The Atlanta Metro area was labyrinthine, and their traffic snarls legendary. It was going to take patience and pluck to start a new life in a region literally fifty times bigger than Knoxville.

Mom was barely through the door when I shared my news.

"I got a call for another interview!" I crowed. "See how easily this is working out? God clearly wants me to go to Atlanta."

"That's great, Heather Pooh."

"I had to tell you before I start studying for my next final."

Mom went to her bedroom to change clothes, and I fired up the Frankencomputer to check my email. Sissy's friend Miller had gifted us a home desktop made from parts of his old ones. It was slow and grinding but came in handy when I was off campus and far from the computer lab.

I logged into my account. An email from Sissy caught my eye. *PLEASE READ – IMPORTANT* read the subject line.

I frowned, wondering what it could be about. Our correspondence was always silly and fun, with subject lines that quoted song lyrics and '80s movies. I hoped everything was ok.

I don't know how to say this. Something has been bothering me about Finn, so I did some investigating. I have bad news. Finn is married to Susannah. I've attached the article so that you can see for yourself. I'm so sorry.
Love, Sissy

My airway shrunk to nothing. I stood up from the chair so quickly, it fell backwards. I rushed to the kitchen counter and fished for my inhaler at the bottom of my purse. My fingers closed around the barrel of it. I pulled off the dust cap and crammed the canister into my mouth, banging my teeth on the edge. The medicine shot into my lungs, and I inhaled deeply. I hoped I would inflate and float away from the horrible email. Instead, my breathing eased, forcing me back to Earth to absorb the shock of what I'd just read.

The download of the article took forever. The age of the computer and the lethargic internet speed in the trailer park made the wait excruciating. Finally, the article loaded, and I clicked on it with trembling hands. It was a year-old write-up from a local alternative weekly, welcoming Finn to town and highlighting his writing career.

The article made mention of Finn and his wife, Susannah, who'd recently relocated from Chicago. Pain slashed my heart as I tried to square what I was reading with what Finn told me. There had to be an explanation.

He said Susannah was gay, I thought in shock. *I'm sure she is, and they're just married on paper for immigration reasons. Or she has a terrible family, and he was trying to protect her. Or they were legit married, and she recently came out to him.*

Surely, it was something like that. Only a psychopath would be married for real and have a profile on a dating site. I studied the picture of Finn and Susannah that accompanied the article. Susannah wasn't pretty, but the way they stood with their arms around each other was loving and intimate and absolutely not platonic.

I briefly compared myself to Susannah but took no comfort from my beauty. In fact, I was sure it didn't matter either way. I recognized the look on Susannah's face because I'd seen it on my own every time I'd been in love: that woman was possessive of what was hers, and what was hers was *Finn*.

"Mama!" I yelled frantically down the hallway. "I need you!"

She was there in a flash.

"Mama," I said as my voice broke, "Finn's married."

"I know, honey," she answered sadly.

"You know?"

"Sissy called me. I wanted to be home when you saw it."

The shame of not discovering the information myself was just starting to burn. I pushed it aside. "I don't understand. Mom, he had a dating profile. He mentioned me on his blog. He's been in love with me for months. Surely, there's an explanation."

I again jumped up from the chair and grabbed my phone, pressing Finn's number to dial him. He didn't answer. The voicemail prompt beeped, and I spoke without thinking.

"Hey, I need you to call me right away, please. I saw something and I want to ask you about it. Ok, talk soon." I paused, and then added, "Love you."

I hung up, no calmer than before. "Mom, what in the *hell* is going on?"

"I don't know, Pooh. Something's been off about him

from the beginning," she said gently. She'd never liked Finn. I knew she was trying hard not to add to my pain by reminding me of it.

Oh God, please don't let them be right about this, I prayed. *I'll die from humiliation.*

"Maybe Susannah is gay, and they're married because he wants to be a U.S. citizen. Or maybe they're separated and not divorced yet."

"Did anything seem off in his house?" Mom asked.

"No. I mean, she had stuff in the bathroom, but that would make sense if they were roommates. There weren't any pictures of them together or any unusual decorations in his bedroom."

Mom inhaled wearily after hearing my last sentence. "*Child,*" she began.

"Don't start. Please," I begged. "This is hard enough as it is."

"Did you look in his closet? Or in the rest of the rooms?"

"No, I did not snoop in his closet. I went into the kitchen, too. That's it."

"Maybe there's an explanation. I hope he'll call soon," said Mom. "Why don't you study for a while, and I'll make us something to eat."

The atmosphere in the trailer had turned funereal. I tried to focus on preparing for my next final. Finn was likely writing or out of town or simply taking a nap. I couldn't let myself be distracted by the sound of the phone not ringing.

I fell into a fitful sleep late in the night. The next morning, I rushed through my final and then went to the computer lab. Finn usually responded to email quickly. I knew that, but the thought had escaped me in the panicked fog of the day before. I sat staring at the blinking cursor, clueless as to what to write. If he was up to no good, I'd have to confirm it over the phone. He'd never admit to it in writing.

After several drafts and countless checks for missed calls, I finally pressed SEND.

> *Hi, my love. Can you please give me a call ASAP? I saw something online that pertains to graduation dates and time is of the essence. Easier to chat than email. Can't wait to see you!*

I didn't have much experience setting traps. The only guile I was presently capable of was putting on a brave face so I wouldn't break down crying. Hopefully, Finn would think I was anxious about hotel reservations or something and call me back right away.

I went home to study for my last two finals. I turned on the Frankencomputer, inviting it to overheat as I constantly refreshed the inbox.

Nothing.

Mom returned from work. She made dinner again since I was too distracted to even pour myself a bowl of cereal. I hunkered down to study. When I was finished, I laid down on the couch and shut my eyes. Tomorrow, as long as I showed up at the right time and put forth a moderate amount of brainpower, I would finally complete my college career, almost eight years after I started.

I should've been deliriously happy, but the raincloud of worry that followed me since yesterday wouldn't dissipate. I showered, watched some TV, and got into bed. I placed my cell phone on the nightstand and left it turned on just in case.

He didn't call.

My last two finals required more concentration than the others. I'd managed to push away all thoughts of Finn until I was flinging open the double doors of the Humanities building after the tests were complete. The day was bright and beautiful. If not for my unanswered questions, I would've run back to my car, screeching with joy the entire way. I'd finished college. *Finally.*

I paused in front of Hodges Library. I felt the warm sun soak into my skin, hoping it would give me a surge of positivity and jump start me into celebration. I thrust my face and chest into a ray unencumbered by the shadows of the building, like a deranged Care Bear. I felt nothing.

I entered the library and trudged to the computer lab. I again emailed Finn.

Hey, is everything ok? Not heard from you in a couple of days and need to firm up some things for graduation. A little worried.

I hadn't considered that there might have been an emergency, and that's why he hadn't called. Maybe he'd been in a car accident or was eaten by mountain lions on the south lawn of Nashville's Parthenon replica. Any reason was better than betrayal.

I went home and waited for Mom. We drove to our favorite South Knoxville restaurant, The Round-Up, for a celebration dinner. We'd been customers since the early '80s, fans of their simple menu and scruffy décor. After ordering at a counter more beat up than the Vols' defensive line, we wedged ourselves into a plastic booth positioned underneath a faded autographed picture of John Ward. I tucked into a burger, while Mom chose a country vegetable plate.

"Honey, I'm so proud of you," she said. "When will they post your grades?"

"Thank you, Mom. I should know in the next day or two."

"Have you heard from Finn?"

I ate a french fry before answering. "No."

"I'm sorry," she said. "When do you go to Atlanta for your interviews?"

"This Friday, I guess. I don't really want to talk about it."

We finished our meal, making sure to wrap up a bite of leftover burger and a smidge of sweet potato casserole for Cookie.

I slept well, all things considered. Before heading to work, I called Finn again. No answer. I sped to my job angrily, barely missing an old lady on a walker as I rounded the corner in front of Food City on Bearden Hill. Whether he was dead or alive, cold-footed or dangerously free-spirited, psychotic or merely inconsiderate, I questioned the timing of it all.

Why had this basket of turds been delivered to me *now?*

As usual, calamity had come stomping up behind, ready to devour my accomplishments whole. If it wasn't poverty, it was illness. If it wasn't illness, it was heartbreak.

"This is BULLSHIT!" I yelled at the top of my lungs. The sound reverberated inside the narrow space of the car, pummeling my eardrums. *"Jesus,"* I added, both as a swear and a prayer.

My anger was only a protective barrier. I knew there were ocean-sized waves of hurt churning underneath the fury. As long as I'd lived, circumstances had never aligned where I'd felt safe, loved, and successful at the same time, but I didn't want to indulge the possibility that it wouldn't *ever* happen. I *couldn't.*

When it was time for my shift, I exited my car to take care of business. The torment would have to wait.

～

ON THURSDAY, I WORKED an early shift and got home mid-afternoon. I turned on the computer as soon as I put down my purse, petting an insistent Cookie with one hand while trying to log onto the student portal with the other. My grades were back.

A, A, A, B.

"Oh, thank *God,*" I exclaimed. I bent down and bonked the dog's head with mine. "Cookie," I said, "I finally did it. I graduated college!" She took a prolonged sniff of my hair and exhaled wetly in congratulations.

"Do you want a baloney sandwich?" I asked. "I want a baloney sandwich."

After celebrating my success with sandwiches, chips, and a leftover Fruit by the Foot brought home from the Karns cafeteria, Cookie and I settled on the couch, awaiting Mom's arrival. I still hadn't heard from my boyfriend, and I was no closer to deciding whether to go to Atlanta for the interviews.

Now that I'd completed college and the show was on hiatus, there was nothing to focus on that wasn't Finn-related. The outlandish soap opera I'd turned on after lunch wasn't nearly enough to silence my thoughts. Finn's capacity to deceive was so potentially enormous that I wasn't sure I'd survive if the worst-case scenario turned out to be true. Surely, he'd get in touch soon, and there would be a good reason for his delay.

Sadness sank into my chest, and I closed my eyes to rest. By the time Mom returned from work, I'd been asleep for two hours.

"Hey, you punkinheads," Mom said. The screen door crashed shut behind her, and I sat up with a start. Cookie flopped down to the floor and lazily greeted Mom, leaving room to stretch out my cramped legs.

"Hey," I replied. "How was your day?"

"I had to work in that nasty dish room. I'm covered in so much food you could put me in the oven and bake me like a casserole. I'm going to take a shower."

"Guess what? I got my grades back. You're looking at a college graduate."

"Baby girl, I'm so proud," Mom said, embracing me despite her need for clean clothes. She smelled of bleach water and rancid animal fat. I returned the hug anyway. She retreated to her bedroom, and I left the couch to grab a soda and refresh the computer.

There were no new emails. The sadness I'd tried to evade during my nap had returned. This time, anger bubbled thickly alongside it. Unless Finn was kidnapped or dead in a ditch somewhere, he would have seen or heard my messages by now. He professed to love me so much that he'd devoted regular time to woo me, had planned to enter the graduation colosseum to meet my bloodthirsty, foreigner-eschewing family, and repeatedly announced intentions to plight his troth. Answering me should have been a priority.

Stupidly, it still made me feel guilty to assume the worst. He was an award-winning author with forty years of successful living under his belt. I was not.

What if he fell off the subway platform in Atlanta and his arms and legs got cut off and he no longer has a way to dial the phone? my mind replied in a panic.

I might've only been a sensitive baby dumpling who barely outran calamity most days, but I was a smart one. The part of me that knew better replied tartly.

Then I guess he better hit those buttons with his nose, girl.

I dialed Finn's number again, ready to leave a scorching voicemail. I knew the voicemail would pick up after four rings, and I needed every second of that time to compose my thoughts.

The phone rang twice. The third ring cut off mid-trill and Finn's message began to play.

I recoiled as if I'd been slapped. He'd rolled me straight to voicemail.

The finality of his answer was unmistakable. I hung up

the phone, stunned. I began to cry. Line after line of tears spilled down my face as my sobs became more guttural.

Mom came running out of her bedroom. "What's wrong?" she asked, alarmed.

"Finn rolled me straight to voicemail, Mama," I sobbed. "He saw it was me calling, and he didn't want to talk."

He'd had every chance to reach out, every benefit of every doubt, and yet Finn had proven himself an odious coward. He was nothing more than a dirty backdoor quack who'd just performed an amputation without anesthetic. My sorrow grew larger, a monstrous thing. I sank onto the loveseat and pulled myself into a fetal position. Mom sat beside me and pulled my head into her lap. She stroked my hair as I grieved.

I cried myself weak. I had almost fallen asleep when I heard my mother ask calmly, "Do you want me to kill him?"

"No!" I sniffed, raising my puffy face to hers. "I'm the one who gets to kill him!"

"I'm sorry this is happening to you, Heather Pooh."

"Mom, why did he suddenly stop talking to me? He didn't know that I'd found the article." I thought through some scenarios. "Is he psychic or something? Did Sissy drive to Nashville and beat his ass without telling me?"

"Not that I know of," answered Mom. "Besides, whoopin' someone isn't Sissy's style. She's more into psychological torture."

"That's true," I said. "She *is* a Scorpio."

"I don't know why he did it, and I don't care. He's a stone-cold bastard as far as I'm concerned. He better hope he never runs into me."

"Mom, what should I do? Finn was the only reason I ever considered Atlanta." If I continued to live in Knoxville, I'd have a place with Dr. A. and hopes for a full-time MAC job. Eventual stagnation, however, was as certain as the kudzu that smothered the city every spring. Did I have the guts to move so far from home?

"Heather, you can stay here – which is fine – or you can go to Atlanta anyway and make a happy life for yourself," she said gently. "Don't let fear keep you trapped here. Don't let some dumbass man be the reason, either. Go, and if it doesn't work out, you can always come back and live with your mama."

I laughed. "That's like telling me that I'm always welcome in county lockup. Not much freedom, but I do get hot meals and a cot to sleep on."

"Hey, what can I say? You can take the girl out of the trailer park, but you can't take the trailer park out of the girl."

Even though it was the most depressing thing she'd ever said to me, her words rang true. "If I find a job in Atlanta, will you help me move?"

"Of course. Who else is going to do it? Cookie?"

Cookie heard her name and took a running leap onto the already crowded loveseat. As soon as she was settled, she began to gnaw noisily on her back. The three of us sat for a while, enjoying the company and drawing comfort from each other's nearness.

∼

GRADUATION DAY ARRIVED WITHOUT incident. Mama, a handful of relatives, and my friend Keke cheered loudly when I walked across the stage at Thompson Boling Arena to receive my diploma. Sissy was busy taking her own finals and couldn't attend. Finn never called back.

I'd paused to pose for my official graduation portrait at the end of the stage, curling my fingers into heavy metal horns instead of shaking hands with the university president. My eyes were covered in orange-and-white glitter in honor of the Vols, and my lips matched my eyes. I wouldn't be ordering any pictures. Official portraits were as much of a money grab as lavish weddings and funerals; any special moment that arose could be captured just as well by a 24-roll of store-brand film and a halfway decent artistic eye.

After the ceremony, Keke and I made plans to meet later for karaoke with the rest of our friends. Mom and I returned to The Round-Up for another quiet celebratory meal. I again ordered their cheeseburger plate, knowing that I wouldn't be back for a long time.

"I'm excited to help you find an apartment," Mom said as we waited for our food. "Don't reckon I've ever been to Atlanta."

My day of interviews had been hectic, but the Town Center cosmetics manager offered me a job at the Shiseido counter on the spot, and I'd accepted.

"I won't actually live in Atlanta," I clarified. "The mall I'll be working at is in Kennesaw, which is north of the city. Navigating traffic is much easier that way." The first time I merged onto the metro's six-lane highway, I thought I might die from fright. Atlanta drivers completely ignored the speed limits. No wonder there were so many jams and complete standstills.

"How do you say the name of where you'll be working?"

"You mean Macy's?" I asked.

Mom scoffed. "No, Punkinhead. Shit-see-do."

"It's pronounced *Shee-say-doe*."

"Whatever."

"I guess this is the last time I'll eat at The Round-Up for a while. Six hours round-trip is a long drive. It's not like when I used to come home every weekend from Kentucky." I took my half-eaten fry and wrote the letters UT in the huge puddle of ketchup on my plate. "I'm going to miss Knoxville, such as it is."

"You girls are old enough and smart enough to do what you want. Knoxville will always be here. You know, I thought I was going to be an overseas missionary after college. I decided to marry your daddy instead. I don't regret it, but I've been stuck here ever since. You need to explore the world and see what happens, baby girl."

Encouragement without envy was Mama's graduation gift to me. She'd done the best she could, carrying me on her shoulders the way countless mothers had lifted countless daughters throughout history. She'd only made it to the edge of the Promised Land. She knew her babies would eventually outpace her and cross the threshold into new abundance.

Love gripped my heart so strongly, tears pricked my eyes. I wouldn't let myself squander her sacrifice.

"I promise, Mama."

"And who knows," she added, "I might move to Georgia myself one of these days."

"*Lord,*" I sighed.

The die was cast; all that was left was to pick a new place to call home. *A second place to call home,* I corrected myself, folding a hunk of cheeseburger into a paper napkin for Cookie. I'd limped along a rocky and meandering road since childhood, fallen on my face a thousand times, and still managed to drag myself across the finish line, wounds and all.

A new set of problems likely awaited in Atlanta or any other place I'd ever live. Whether there was Someone guiding my steps or not, trouble had a way of finding me. If I didn't stay strong, I might drop dead from despair and my sorrowful remains bulldozed over for a tacky new shopping center.

But I was ready. Just because I kept getting kicked into holes didn't mean that I had to wallow at the bottom. In the future, when I was weary and needed rest, I'd look at the dirt packed along the edges of my torn, stinging cuticles and remind myself.

I wouldn't let life keep a good woman – or even an unrepentantly stubborn one — down.

BIG CHICKEN

Usually, the gentle whirl of prolonged interstate travel left me snoring against the plastic edge of the passenger side door. This morning, I was too excited to sleep. Mom and I had left Knoxville at sunrise, stopping at Weigel's for coffee and steak biscuits before hitting the road.

Stacked on top of the emergency brake was a map of the Atlanta metro area and a thick sheaf of printed MapQuest directions. When we'd driven across the state line into Georgia, we'd cheered and beeped the horn wildly, on a mission to find an apartment and help me stake my claim in the big city.

Our first stop was Town Center Mall, where I'd been hired as Macy's sole Shiseido representative. Town Center was nicely sized and suburban, landing somewhere between Knoxville's East and West Town Malls in terms of fanciness. For now, I was thrilled to be a one-woman show. It seemed the perfect place to dip my toes into the metro career pool.

We drove around Kennesaw, looking at a couple of apartment complexes I'd researched. None were quite right. My budget was modest, as always, and I needed to keep my finances flexible for the possibility of cute dresses and nights out. Marietta was directly south of Kennesaw, and we decided to head there after exhausting all the possibilities around the mall. We turned onto Cobb Parkway to explore.

I felt strong and confident. Georgia was welcoming us with bright sunshine. The metro area, even twenty miles from Atlanta proper, buzzed with the shiny energy of innovation and modernization. Buildings were prettier here than in Knoxville, where a dull lack of polish covered the entire city like dandruff. People were more polite than back home, too, surprising us at Walmart where we'd stopped for a six-pack of cheap, unrefrigerated soft drinks. We'd also discovered that food was barely taxed in Georgia. In Tennessee, we were taxed like we'd landed on a Monopoly square stacked with hotels, watching hard-earned money disappear from our pockets and funneled into so-called rainy-day funds, never to be seen again.

The potential for good things made my stomach twist eagerly. I had an important task to complete before I left Knoxville. The shock of Finn's betrayal had worn off just enough to start planning. My last official act as a Tennessean would be to print copies of the emails he'd sent me, highlight each declaration of love and fidelity, and mail them to his wife.

As we drove along Cobb Parkway, I pictured Susannah opening the package addressed to her and reading Finn's emails in horror. After his confession, I saw her burning his ugly black jeans and the rest of his wardrobe while simultaneously booking a consultation with a divorce attorney.

The thought of his dumb jazz fest t-shirts ablaze in their trendy clawfoot tub would keep me warm on even the coldest Georgia nights – I was sure of it.

I knew I'd never receive an apology, and there was a good chance that he'd intercept the package anyway, but at least I'd rattle him to his questionably talented core. The cad had tried to ignore me into submission. I would not be silenced.

Mom interrupted my reverie. "Are there any apartments around here?"

I checked my stack of printouts. "Yes, several. We should be coming up on some in a few minutes. This is a long road. We could drive it all the way into downtown Atlanta if we wanted to."

"Anything to get off that interstate for a while. Are you sure you can handle the traffic around here?" Mom asked.

"Only one way to find out. You know, I think I'm going to like Atlanta."

We continued down Cobb Parkway, commenting on the range of businesses along its corridor.

"Hey, there's a waterpark!" I said, pointing to Mom's left.

"You don't even like waterparks," Mom scoffed. "Do they have Shoney's down here?"

"It's a major metropolitan area. Of course they do."

"A place ain't civilized if they don't got Shoney's. Remember that."

I looked at the map. "We're supposed to turn at the next intersection. There's another complex not too far from here. Looks promising."

Mom slowed down as she reached the traffic light. The car's brakes squeaked slightly as we came to a stop.

"What in the *hell* is that?" Mom exclaimed.

On the corner of Cobb Parkway and Roswell Road, a five-story Chicken stood tall. The giant bird lay affixed atop a KFC, announcing to all within its massive wingspan that delicious chicken was, in fact, available in the building below its monstrous visage.

"It's a restaurant," I said in awe.

The beak of the Big Chicken opened and closed endlessly while motorized eyes never circled in the same direction.

"Mom," I said, "I must live near this chicken."

I knew I would be safe under its psychotic gaze. I felt the Chicken understood the darkest parts of the human heart. I saw my future reflected in the eatery's sparkling glass doors, clearer than a brand-new crystal ball. After a long day of working at the mall, I would drive home, park under its gaping mechanized maw, and enjoy my revenge and newfound freedom as I licked mashed potatoes off a spork.

"I always knew there was something wrong with Colonel Sanders," Mom said with a shake of her head.

Mom and I pulled into a small apartment complex a few streets over from the Big Chicken. We met the property manager, whom I liked, and toured a small one-bedroom apartment that was decent but painfully plain, reminding me of home.

"This is it," I told Mom. "This is where I'm going to live."

"I think it's a neat little place," she said, opening each cabinet and drawer in the kitchen and sniffing deeply. "I don't smell any mold or too much bug spray. You're close to work, too. Are you ready to sign a lease?"

A million things could go wrong, like they usually did. Already, my heart began to palpitate in anticipation of being so far away from her. I swallowed hard to get rid of the lump in my throat.

"God wouldn't have made things work out so easily if He didn't want me to be here, right?"

It didn't seem to matter whether I planned extensively

or just jumped feet first into something new. Things tended to work out – sort of – either way.

Mom acknowledged what I'd said with a nod. "I'd like to think so, baby girl." She had decades of experience with her mercurial Creator. Experience wasn't the same as knowledge. "Give it your best shot. That's all you can do."

"Do you ever think about what you'd say to God if you met Him face to face?"

"Not specifically, no. He's got a lot of explaining to do, though." Mama finished her inspection of the apartment with a long inhale inside the refrigerator. "Smells clean," she said, satisfied.

"I guess it's time to sign the lease," I said, folding my hand into hers like I did when I was a little girl.

"I'll tell you one thing," Mom began, "when I do meet God, that'll mean I'm dead and can finally get some rest. I haven't had a good night's sleep since your daddy went to Heaven."

My mother was the ultimate reigning champion of the 1-2 uplift-punch combination, a move so emotionally lethal it was banned in some countries.

"Sorry to hear that, Mama," I answered with a resigned sigh.

"I'll be fine, Heather," she said, flicking her free hand as if her revelation was of little importance, "and so will you."

Together, we walked carefully down the flight of concrete stairs to the leasing office to make things official. Mama's most sensitive and evolutionarily challenged baby bird was ready for takeoff. Even though I was leaving my whole support system behind in Tennessee, I'd find something here to take me under its wing — God, the Universe, or perhaps the gigantic mechanical rooster that was within walking distance of my new apartment.

My flight pattern had been choppy, and I'd returned to the nest an embarrassing number of times, but in a new place, free from reminders of the past, I again had the chance to soar.

AUTHOR BIO

HEATHER REAM wants you to know that you'll be ok. Heather is a progressive Christian and the proud owner of a twangy Appalachian accent. She lives with her husband and a delusional amount of optimism in Knoxville, TN.